Art 7–11

Curriculum in primary practice series
General editor: Clive Carré

The Curriculum in primary practice series is aimed at students and qualified teachers looking to improve their practice within the context of the National Curriculum. The large format, easy to use texts are interactive, encouraging teachers to engage in professional development as they read. Each contains:

- Summaries of essential research
- Transcripts of classroom interactions for analysis and discussion
- Activities for individual and group use

While all primary teachers will find these books useful, they are designed with the needs of teachers of the 7 to 11 age group particularly in mind.

Other titles include:

Science 7–11
Clive Carré and Carrie Ovens

Drama 7–11
Neil Kitson and Ian Spiby

Music 7–11
Sarah Hennessy

History 7–11
Jon Nichol with Jacqui Dean

Religious Education 7–11
Terence Copley

Art 7–11

Developing primary teaching skills

Linda Green and Robin Mitchell

ROUTLEDGE

London and New York

First published 1997
by Routledge
11 New Fetter Lane, London EC4P 4EE

Simultaneously published in the USA and Canada
by Routledge
29 West 35th Street, New York, NY 10001

Typeset in Palatino by Solidus (Bristol) Limited
Printed and bound in Great Britain by Butler and Tanner

British Library Cataloguing in Publication Data
A catalogue record for this book is available from the British Library

Library of Congress Cataloging in Publication Data
Green, Linda.
    Art 7–11 : developing primary teaching skills / Linda Green and
        Robin Mitchell
    p. cm. — (Curriculum in primary practice)
    Includes bibliographical references and index.
    1. Art—Study and teaching (Primary) 2. Art teachers—Training
        of. I. Mitchell, Robin. II. Title. III. Series.
    N350.G72   1997
    372.5—dc20   96-28531
                                                            CIP

ISBN 0–415–12841–2

Contents

Illustrations

The colour plate section appears between pages 64 and 65.

COLOUR PLATES

FIGURES

Acknowledgements

We should like to thank all those teachers, children, students and colleagues who have helped us write this book. In their particular ways they represent the educational community and within our work we have endeavoured to focus attention on those matters which have a common purpose to all of these parties. We regard ourselves and our teacher colleagues as fellow learners with the students and children with whom we work. Underpinning this book is an ethos which we hope reflects a co-operative spirit and an openness toward learning about art, and about the ways in which this subject is a powerful means of making sense of the world. In particular we are indebted to the following people, who through their work gave us inspiration and throughout their efforts made this endeavour possible. To Linda Dawe, Wes Hall, and the children of Landscore Primary School for their help and lovely art work; similarly to Gini Wells and the teachers and children at Ottery St Mary Primary School. To Joseph and the other children in London, Devon and Avon and to Alan Richards for his wisdom and paintings. To Jonathan Mitchell for his photography and Jackie Edwards for her patient secretarial support.

We are indebted to the following for permission to reproduce works of art: the Corcoran Gallery, Washington, USA, for Plate 3; the Musée du Louvre, Paris, for Plate 2; the Musée D'Orsay, Paris, for Plate 1 and the Reina Sofia Art Centre, Madrid, for Figure 2.2. We are grateful also to HarperCollins Publishers for permission to quote from: *The Arts in the Primary School*, R. Taylor and G. Andrews; *Teaching Art to Young Children*, Rob Barnes; and *Feeling and Reason in the Arts*, David Best.

And finally to our students – we hope the book will be of use.

Introduction

What does art mean to primary children? What does art mean to their teachers? How do children and teachers learn to understand, appreciate and make art, and what language is it necessary to develop in order to be able to talk about it? These are the key questions addressed by this book.

For children, art might mean painting or working with clay; designing and printing Christmas cards or making a collage; making a model from junk materials or sewing a toy animal; weaving a mat or visiting a gallery. Art means many things to primary children, and to their teachers. Our aim is to help you enhance your understanding of and practice in art, both by drawing on your considerable knowledge of the children you teach and becoming involved in activities with your colleagues and the children in your class. We hope that the activities in this book will enable you to answer with confidence the question of what art might mean to primary children, and to plan an exciting and appropriate art curriculum with your colleagues.

Primarily, for children art means drawing. It would be difficult to find a primary classroom devoid of paper and pencils, and given access to these materials most children will draw. They like to draw. They choose to draw. Children draw in moments of spare time; in wet play times; at dinner time; in lessons when asked and when they should be doing something else. They draw in their sketch books and rough books; they decorate the covers of their work books and text book margins, the playground surfaces and the lavatory walls.

Why?

Because they like drawing.

Why?

Because it seems to satisfy some basic need to communicate about what they know of themselves and their world, to express feelings or describe their experience. And importantly, because it is a vital part of their peer and school culture. As soon as a child makes the first representational drawing and names it, he or she has joined in a commonly

Painting pictures and making models are part of what art can be

understood activity. All cultures yield examples of drawing – the prehistoric cave paintings from Lascaux and Altamira; Aboriginal images and native American art; the Egyptian hieroglyphs and geometric Greek pot decoration – all demonstrate the human need to communicate through drawing. We understand each other's drawings; they communicate with us, now and across time, about others. Young children producing their first drawings receive immediate confirmation from siblings, parents, relatives or, within the school, their peers and teachers. For some children drawing precedes speech; for most children it certainly precedes the written word.

The remarkable feature about drawing, which should fascinate and interest us as teachers, is that children are framing their own learning in an authentic activity that has high personal value and meaning. The child's identification with the drawing is usually strong. The activity, set in motion by the child, results in an image that is socially available because others can take meaning from it and as such it becomes part of the context of ordinary communication.

The really remarkable event of a child entering into this personally satisfying and socially acceptable activity is taken very much for granted, because of its 'ordinariness'. It is recognised that the developing language of a child becomes more elaborated with age and experience so that, in time, more complicated ideas can be expressed. So, too, in art is it possible to consider the elaboration of drawing in a similar way, and this is dealt with in detail in Unit 4.

Underpinning the discussion and suggestions in this book are the findings from two important research projects. The first, the Leverhulme Primary Project, based at the University of Exeter's School of Education, involved a national survey of over nine hundred primary teachers in 1989 (Wragg, Bennett and Carré 1989). They were asked to state how competent they felt to teach the National Curriculum with their existing subject knowledge. As expected, teachers thought themselves to be most competent in English (81 per cent of the sample), whereas in art only 48 per cent indicated that they were competent. All the teachers indicated that they needed support in this subject.

Part of the research programme in this project involved assessing student-teachers' subject knowledge, and the extent to which this knowledge affected their classroom performance (Bennett and Carré 1993: 17–46). Data from this project, and from other research, indicate the importance of 'subject knowledge for teaching' (as opposed to subject knowledge in itself) in order to enhance teaching performance and the quality of teaching.

The second research initiative, the Critical Studies in Art Education Project (CSAE 1981–84) was sponsored by the Arts Council, the Crafts Council, the Schools Council and subsequently by the School Curriculum Development Committee. It was directed by Rod Taylor, who was at that time the Art Advisor for Wigan Education Authority and Director of the Drumcroon Education Art Centre. The research originated from a growing realisation that much art teaching solely emphasised practical work, and the traditional teaching of 'art history', where it existed, generally lacked discernible effect on children's work. Consequently, the 'contemplative aspects of art education had virtually disappeared' (Taylor 1986). The research showed that there was a need for teachers to develop sound subject knowledge for teaching, and further, for children to study critically the work of art and artists as a means of developing the expressive power of their own art making.

The research and development of art teaching in schools carried out under Taylor's direction very substantially influenced the subsequent direction of British art education, and underpinned much of the thinking behind the development of the National Curriculum for Art between 1990 and 1995.

In our own current research, in which we are conducting surveys with 250 student teachers and teachers about their arts teaching in schools, the preliminary findings indicate similar results to the above. Only half of the student teachers surveyed felt that they were able to learn about art from a class teacher and even then the advice was about the classroom management of pupils, resources and materials. Less than a third of the students felt they were able to learn subject knowledge for teaching from a class teacher. These findings are now being broadly confirmed through interviews with teachers. What is emerging from the interviews is a low level of teacher confidence in their own subject knowledge in teaching art and some uncertainty about children's learning in and through art.

Thus, from these lines of empirical work and from our extensive knowledge of practice in a variety of schools, we have in this book a triple emphasis:

- on knowledge and understanding of art by *the teacher*;
- and equally, on the need for *children* to be knowledgeable, by studying the work of other artists, to help develop their own art making;
- further, for teachers to support children's learning in art with an adequate understanding of the way children develop in art.

In carrying out research for this book we have talked to teachers, student teachers, children and artists in order to illuminate concerns and identify key issues. We have also tested certain ideas to support teacher subject knowledge for teaching in the classroom and evaluated the results with teachers and children.

Throughout the book we suggest strategies for setting up activities that allow teachers opportunities to observe children at work. These activities centre on key areas and stages of children's development which inform us about their knowledge and understanding of art.

We emphasise the benefit of observing the ideas and methods of artists past and present. Further, we suggest the importance of observing and reflecting on our own practice as art makers. We stress the importance of student teachers and teachers making works of art for themselves. It is not necessary to be a great artist in order to teach art well, but it does help to have first-hand experience to draw upon. Teachers need to develop a sensitivity to an appropriate range of different materials used in art, craft and design in primary schools. Practice and reflection on this practice, with experience, will facilitate better organisation of materials, understanding of processes and class management. This will enable teachers to maximise the delights and reduce the potential pitfalls of pupils making their own works of art.

However, central to the success of both teachers' work and that of pupils is a knowledge and understanding of art through the critical study of artists' work. There is available to teachers and children a rich reservoir of material to stimulate, inform and provide comparative examples. We hold that observing the practice of professional artists, first-hand or through films, videos or books about artists, can offer authentic experience to primary pupils and their teachers about art making.

Strategies are suggested to enable teachers and students to look at art analytically in the classroom with their pupils. Teachers and students can further increase their knowledge and understanding of the subject through visits to art galleries and museums, where they can 'interrogate' and analyse works of art first-hand, and learn from them. These strategies will enable non-specialists to become active observers and enter into a dialogue with the artist. This dialogue will necessarily include teachers' own perceptions of both art and life experience, which in turn may be modified and changed in the light of this encounter.

Rod Taylor gives an example of this change in perception in a case study of Lydia who visited an art gallery, the Courtauld Institute, with her parents when she was 10 years old:

 I saw a Seurat painting and I was amazed at the effect that was given with the dots, all the colours merging together, and the kind of soft overall appearance that was given because of the use of dots with no harsh lines or edges.

(Taylor 1986: 18)

The memorable effect of that visit was to influence her secondary education, her work in art school and her work as an art teacher. Lydia explains that she is conscious of the significance of that visit for her work as artist and teacher:

 I've never really got over the impact of Seurat. No matter how many other artists I do get a strong feeling for – for instance, sometimes I go through a phase of liking Van Eyck's work, or I go on to somebody else and for a while I'm just looking at books with their work in, Gustav Klimt or whoever – but I always seem to have this strong feeling for Seurat as well. I never seem to have lost that respect for Seurat's work or the great enjoyment that I've always got out of it.

(Taylor 1986: 19)

Lydia has returned to a close scrutiny of this artist's work over a good number of years. This ever-questioning dialogue is Socratic in nature and based on what Peter Abbs calls 'the ordinary nature of the aesthetic', our understanding through the senses. Our understanding must find an appropriate voice in order to describe our aesthetic response. Abbs suggests:

 The grammar of the arts, therefore, cannot be introduced through a series of prescribed schematic exercises divorced from the animating energies of feelings, sense, perception and imagination. They must be introduced as a necessary part of *expressive activity seeking formal articulation.* ... The knowledge of the symbolic field is best imparted through direct aesthetic engagement with many different genres, through an imaginative involvement with their meanings. ... The art teacher's task is to promote that reciprocal play between the repertoire of artistic conventions inherited through the culture and that innate proclivity in the individual and group for symbolic expression.

(Abbs 1989: 38–9)

Our task is to support primary teachers and students in finding ways of understanding and then supporting this reciprocal interplay.

This book links art theory and practice, seeking to dispel the idea that one is separate from the other. Art for primary children, and for us all, is an act of enquiry, but is also a way of understanding our experience and that of others, and in practice is a way of making explicit our selves and our beliefs. A study of art works by other artists will in turn reveal something of the traditions and culture of that person.

The book is organised into the following seven units:

Unit 1 discusses the nature of art; outlines the range of artefacts and processes normally included, and draws some distinctions between art, craft and design.

Unit 2 is concerned with establishing a subject knowledge base in art to facilitate teaching, including consideration of National Curriculum attainment targets.

Unit 3 focuses on models for children's process of learning in art and teachers' strategies, grounded in reflective practice, to support that learning.

Unit 4 discusses children and their art – the development apparent in their art making and art appreciation.

Unit 5 discusses models for planning a variety of programmes of work, each with a different emphasis and starting point, in order to support the curriculum strategies of different schools.

Unit 6 proposes structured programmes of practical activities to support classroom teaching, including critical study, formal artistic elements, visual literacy and National Curriculum requirements, together with aspects of assessment. Importance is given to the authenticity of the child's own voice in the formative and summative assessment of their own work.

Unit 7 concludes with some further thoughts on art in the primary curriculum, and reviews ways of developing professional confidence through building subject knowledge and reflection on authentic practice.

DIFFERENT WAYS OF USING THIS BOOK

Read about it – a topic, an issue, an idea.
Do it – a practical activity or a discussion.
Talk about it – review and analyse what has been carried out and discussed.
Plan – develop strategies for future action.
Do some more!

Works of art referred to in the text

You will be asked to consider several works of art in the teacher activities and schemes of work, and if you are not familiar with the artists' work it will be important for you to have reproductions to refer to. Some works are illustrated in this book; those artists referred to but not illustrated are listed below so that you can find books containing the work in the local library.

Works by these artists can be found in most general histories of art or modern art, but in particular in the following books: E.H. Gombrich (1995, 16th edition) *The Story of Art*, Phaidon Press Ltd; R. Hughes (1991) *The Shock of the New*, BBC Publications.

Reproductions, including postcards, can also be obtained from galleries and museums or from Shorewood Educational (see Resources section, page 135).

Unit 1

The cave paintings at Lascaux.
Auguste Rodin (1840–1917) *The gates of hell*
Jean Tinguely (1928–91) Kinetic sculptures
Jean François Millet (1814–75) *The Angelus*

Unit 2

Pieter Bruegel (1525/30–69) *Children's games*
Rembrandt van Rijn (1606–69) and L.S. Lowry (1887–1976) drawings and paintings of people
Paul Gauguin (1848–1903) *Hail Mary*
Hendrik Avercamp (1585–1634) *Winter Scene*
Claude Monet (1840–1926) *The Gare St-Lazare*
Giacomo Balla (1871–1958) 'Dynamism of a dog on a leash'/'Speeding auto'
Umberto Boccioni (1827–1901) drawings of cyclists

Unit 5

'Ourselves'

Henri Matisse (1869–1954), Vincent van Gogh (1853–1890), Rembrandt van Rijn (1606–69)
– line/tone drawings
Pop Art (1960s) – colour and detail
Marc Chagall (1887–1985), Giorgio de Chirico (1888–1978) – references to memory, dreams
Henry Moore (1898–1986) – family groups

'The home and school environment'

Jan Vermeer (1632–75), Pieter de Hooch (1629–1684), Giorgio Canaletto (1697–1761) –
drawings, detail (bricks, tiles, windows)
Anthony Green (*b.* 1939) – architectural drawings, paintings
The Boyle Family – paintings and relief castings
Barbara Hepworth (1903–1975) and Ben Nicholson (1894–1982) – shape, form, texture,
pattern
Medieval and Celtic art – pattern
John Constable (1776–1837), Lowry, Carel Weight (*b.* 1908) – mood, colour and tone
W.P. Frith (1819–1909) *Paddington Station*

'The wider world – work and play'

Van Gogh (1853–1890) *Sower* and Georges Seurat (1859–91) *Sower*
David Hockney (*b.* 1937) and Leon Kossof (*b.* 1926) – swimming pool pictures
Matisse (1869–1954) – *Swimmers* series

Unit 6

Millet (1814–75) *The Gleaners*
Monet (1840–1926) and Paul Cézanne (1839–1906)

For teachers working with colleagues in school

You may decide to read this book and develop your own understanding of art through the
ideas and suggested activities. Built into the text are teacher activities, and it is suggested
that these are mostly shared with a colleague. There is an assumption that discussing
matters is of great benefit and can illuminate some of the issues, and expose misunderstandings and prejudices. It is very important to demystify some of the elements of the subject,
and the aim is to promote understanding and enjoyment of art and the development of
professional expertise and confidence in teaching it.

For in-service and professional studies courses

The text in this book can be used in several ways:
Read about it – group discussion of ideas and issues raised within the Units.
Do it – individual or collaborative experiments with practical activities in the classroom.
Talk about it – in whole school meetings, reflect on practice, supported by further reading of sections of the Units.
Plan further action – individual or collaborative planning to build on teaching experiences and children's learning.

The following symbols are used throughout the book to denote:

   quotations from published materials

   activities

✳   transcripts of children and/or teachers talking

What counts as art? Developing an understanding of the subject

In early November 1992 Julian Champkin, writing in the *Daily Mail*, reported:

> This week, the organisers of London's biggest art fair which opens today polled 1,000 men and women in the street. Passers by were asked to name a well-known artist and then the votes were added up.

Quite a question, if you are not expecting it. Who comes to mind? Maybe Van Gogh? Would Monet get a look in, or if not, surely Rembrandt would? Not at all. The result was very unexpected:

> Some of the world's greatest artistic geniuses got less than 5% of the vote – Rembrandt, for instance, and Francis Bacon. Turner did better with 14%, Constable very well with 23%. But the winner, with 38%, was the real surprise. It was the popular Australian, Rolf Harris.

Shock!! Horror!! More people have heard of Rolf Harris than Rembrandt. What a terrible indictment against the effectiveness of English art education, that it failed to instil in the memory of the average London pedestrian any knowledge of art and artists. This may be so, but more importantly we need to know why the majority of respondents thought of Harris. He is a picture maker, a performer, a person who can demonstrate the ability to conjure up an image with a few deft brushstrokes. There is an element of magic about his artistic TV performances – his brushstrokes initially give the viewer few clues to the image, but before the viewer's very eyes the magic works and the picture falls into place like some miraculous vision. The wizard has performed his trick and behold, the result.

The artist as magician has a very ancient lineage, from the cave paintings of Lascaux, mask-making and tribal dancing from all cultures, to the multi-media and sometimes exploding kinetic sculpture of Tinguely. Somehow an element of this magic still survives. No matter how much of a cliché the pictorial image may be, the result still stirs in the spectator a sense of wonder at the demonstration of skill which is beyond that of the spectator. To be really successful for present-day onlookers, whatever image or picture is being constructed, it must strike a chord of recognition, identification and understanding.

TRADITIONS, IMAGES AND SYMBOLS

The philosopher David Best proposes, 'in the most fundamental sense, the meaning of the arts, as of language, is rooted in human actions and responses and cultural practices' (Best 1992: 16).

All works of art draw on human actions and cultural practices. They are a particular kind of response made by an artist working within a set of cultural traditions. The art work subsequently becomes a new addition to that culture. In order to identify with a work of art the spectator must be able to place it within his or her own previous experience of what they understand as art. This art may be within a genre – for example many of Rolf Harris' illustrations will correspond to the spectator's memory of Walt Disney's images. Both sets of images are easy to understand, and they carry a straightforward emotional charge. They are often sentimental and relate to a world that exists within the imagination but also refer to some touchstones of human experience, for example the complexity of feeling which surrounds our relationship with the natural and animal worlds.

However, other easily recognisable symbols signify meanings and associations beyond the simple form of their illustration. For example, the crucifix and the Coca-Cola bottle are icons which are readily understood by the population at large, albeit at different levels. Consider the crucifix. The manner and range of its use is extensive. It may appear as a decorative and superficial adjunct to fashion, but in contrast denotes the whole complexity of Christian thought and faith. Similarly, the Coca-Cola bottle may illustrate the product itself but can also represent or symbolise the content and style of modern American capitalist culture. These cultural icons are part of the childhood and everyday lives of many people. Commercial advertising regularly uses simple, commonly recognisable images to convey more complex messages and stimulate emotional responses in their recipients. This is the stuff of everyday life, but it also indicates a central concern of art education.

The result of the survey mentioned earlier, and similar evidence, gives rise to much anxiety on the part of many art educators. Rod Taylor, in the introduction to his seminal work *Educating for Art*, lists a number of major anxieties which were being increasingly expressed about art education. Two principle issues were:

> 1 There was a growing concern that the emphasis on practical work in many schools had become so dominant that the contemplative aspects of art education had virtually disappeared.
> 2 The majority of art teachers had rejected the art history lecture as a means of giving pupils an understanding of the visual arts and of art and craft objects.
>
> (Taylor 1986: xi)

Can the *Daily Mail* survey be seen as further evidence to suggest that our efforts to educate the population about the visual arts and the world's greatest artists has come to nothing? This may be the case, but it is possible to take a less pessimistic view. When asked to name a 'well-known artist' what the people in the survey may have had in their minds was the practical processes and craft skills of making art, not necessarily the quality of the 'artist's' picture. We suspect that a different question, asking people to identify a picture rather than an artist, would have elicited *The Hay Wain*, the *Mona Lisa*, David Shepherd's paintings of charging elephants, or various paintings by Renoir and Monet. We may therefore speculate that most people's knowledge of art relates to two separate but related things, artefacts and artists. We recognise certain artefacts as being 'art', for example a painting in a friend's sitting room or a marble sculpture of a reclining figure in an art gallery. We recognise the ceramics, woven hangings and prints on sale at craft fairs as 'art' and acknowledge the graphic design of posters as art work. Secondly, we acknowledge that artists make these objects.

There is another interesting factor at work here that may have influenced the respondents. Some artists, by the very nature of their work, are innovative and produce novel, original ideas which challenge our view of the world and ways of looking at things. This challenge presents problems for us as onlookers and often our understanding of contemporary artefacts is severely limited. It seems to take society a while to develop the understanding necessary to relate to the work. An example of this is the way in which the work of the Impressionists was initially received. In the late nineteenth century the work outraged the critics and aroused derision and scorn; yet now we delight in the works of Monet and Renoir and recognise their worth.

The fact that some new art is difficult to understand may explain why for most people modernist twentieth century art in almost any form is suspect – hence the choice of Rolf Harris rather than, say, Francis Bacon.

A further factor that can 'distance' art from everyday life is the prevailing view that artists behave in unusual ways and do not live in the 'real' world. This stems partly from nineteenth century legend, constructed around artists like Van Gogh and Gauguin, but mostly it is based on a deeper and more ancient myth, that of the artist as magician and priest. Gombrich speculates about the artist in this role when discussing the cave paintings at Lascaux:

 The most likely explanation of these finds is still that they are the oldest relics of that universal belief in the power of picture-making; in other words, that these primitive hunters thought that if they only made a picture of their prey – and perhaps belaboured it with their spears or stone axes – the real animals would also succumb to their power.

(Gombrich 1972: 22)

One of the purposes of art education is to start with popular opinion and develop from that a raft of understandings about art, through considering the nature of art and the lives of artists. This will bring about increased awareness, and, combined with practical art making, may create a deeper understanding of the subject in its cultural and historical context. It will enable the learner to make personal, meaningful art work and also to employ ways of representing significant events and feelings which share a common language with great artists.

In order to explore this notion and to help you make connections between your everyday life experiences and the world of art, find a colleague to do the following activity with you.

TEACHER ACTIVITY 1.1

'Reading' a picture

Plates 1 and 2 show two works by famous artists, *A dance at the Moulin de la Galette* by Renoir and *The raft of the Medusa* by Géricault.

1   Regarding the subject matter, what do you think the picture is about?
2   What are the main artistic devices that the artist has used (such as line, colour, shape, form, texture, pattern, tone)? Think also about the predominant colour scheme, types of brushstrokes, use of light and shade, and composition.
3   What atmosphere does the picture convey?
4   How does the picture make you feel?

After responding to these two pictures you may conclude that one is about happiness and the other about disaster. Judging by most pictures on display in high street stores, it could be concluded that all pictures are about happy events, pleasant atmosphere and harmonious colour. These reproduction prints reflect the contemporary preference for lighthearted paintings. Other art forms, especially novels and films, are often most popular when they deal with the darker side of life, such as murder, disaster and conflict.

Figure 1.1 Working on a painting

The whole business of taste and reaction to works of art can vary according to our pre-conceptions about what is suitable subject matter and also how these different art forms interface with our everyday life. An additional aspect in considering our reaction to works of art is the extent we engage with them in private or in public; whether they can be returned to at leisure such as a painting or a book, or are of a transitory nature such as a play or musical concert. Most paintings are public. They have been made for exhibition in religious or public buildings, galleries and homes. In education we are concerned with a whole range of subject matter relating to the human condition and the work may, in some cases, be unpleasant or difficult to come to terms with.

'I DON'T KNOW ANYTHING ABOUT ART BUT I KNOW WHAT I LIKE!'

This well-worn cliché has some resonance for us all. So, what do we like? How does what we like relate to what we know about art? How does an increased knowledge about art influence what we like?

 TEACHER ACTIVITY 1.2

The following text is a conversation with Susan, who is 10 years old. She had been talking about artists she admires and about her liking for Picasso. She was then told about Rolf Harris being named as a well-known artist and asked if she knew who he was:

Susan   Yes, he still draws pictures but they are completely different from Picasso's.

Interviewer   Different in what way?

Susan   They are more cartoony ... I think if there was more than one category, like there was a cartoon artist category, he would go top of the cartoon artist category.

Susan puts forward the idea that artists and works of art can be put in categories. It may be that by so doing we can make it easier to define what art is.

Look at the images illustrated in Figure 1.2. Try to group these images together so that they form categories – for example, cartoons, adverts, famous paintings, etc.

When you have a satisfactory arrangement, list the images accordingly. Discuss or write down the reasons for choosing the categories and also reasons for including particular images in them.

 TEACHER ACTIVITY 1.3

1   Ask a friend or colleague to do Activity 1.2. Has your colleague categorised the images in a different way to you?

2   Consider the following statement with your colleague, exploring the reasons for your choices. This will involve you in discussing both the content of art and the visual elements used in making them.

    Statement: There is no *one* right way of categorising these images. In doing this activity we construct and categorise the images according to our previous knowledge, experience and understanding.

3   Talk about the fact that art fulfils different purposes, in different contexts. For example, Michelangelo's *David* is quite different from the Superhero figure, although both represent some sort of ideal of manhood (the hero). They are different in style and in how they make the viewer feel.

Figure 1.2 Images to categorise

LIKING, KNOWING AND MAKING

The above activity involved you in talking about your ideas of art and what you know about art. We need to consider to what extent liking and knowing about art influences the making of works of art. To put it another way, does a knowledge of what other artists have done over the centuries help a person create more effective pieces of sculpture or paint better pictures? Our stance is that knowing about what has gone before should help us in developing new ideas. Nobody would question the notion of a developing tradition in science or engineering, but sometimes in the arts this assumption is questioned.

Both in the arts and in science the development of new ideas is concerned with leaps of the imagination, but these 'leaps' also draw upon past influences. For example, Rodin's late-nineteenth century sculpture, 'The thinker' (1880), a seminal work from 'The gates of hell' commissioned by the Museum of Decorative Arts in Paris as entrance doors for the museum, bridges the nineteenth and twentieth centuries. It indicates a new way of thinking about sculpture which was influential on later twentieth century work by artists such as Brancusi and Henry Moore. It symbolises a democratic view of man as creator and guardian of his own destiny.

The form of 'The thinker' derives partly from Michelangelo but also from Rodin's extensive first-hand drawing of moving figures. In the figure of the thinker, the narrative and symbolic elements that are used to portray the figure as God (strength, age, wisdom and compassion) are also designed to indicate an 'Everyman' figure contemplating the human predicament in judging the complexities of good and evil. The design of the sculpture and its surroundings are also based on the fifteenth century artist Lorenzo Ghiberti's great bronze doors of the Baptistry in Florence, and draw on images from Dante's poem *The inferno* and poets of Rodin's own time, such as Baudelaire. All these influences combine to produce this brooding figure, which has become a modern icon.

The notion that a knowledge of art history and tradition helps artists to develop their own work is party addressed by the National Curriculum for Art (DFE 1995). Through its interlinking attainment targets, 'investigating and making' and 'knowledge and understanding', the National Curriculum makes explicit the relationship between the pupils' knowledge of art, its history, traditions and artists, and the children's ability to make new works of art.

ART, CRAFT AND DESIGN

It is necessary to reach some broad definition of what the term 'art' embraces in the context of education, in order to be clear about the specific sorts of 'art' children are expected to learn about. The National Curriculum defines 'art' thus: 'Art should be interpreted as "art, craft and design" throughout' (DFE 1995: 2). On the face of it this all-emcompassing definition seems convenient, but it is clear that a painting is different from a pot or the design of an aeroplane.

Some of the similarities and differences between art, craft and design will need to be teased out. This may help to elicit some common understandings which in turn may enable the teacher to devise more appropriate activities for children.

Looking for differences

What factors distinguish art, from craft, from design? It may be helpful to look first at the differences in terms of the maker's intentions. The intention of the artist, in a very general sense, might be characterised by a concern with making imagery based on personal ideas, thoughts or feelings about experience and the human condition. Sometimes this imagery flies in the face of what is currently acceptable; it may shock and lead to criticism of the artist.

In the following passage the French nineteenth century painter Millet, whose painting *The Angelus* shows workers pausing in their work in the fields to pray, defends his right to paint the scenes of peasant life and labours that were the background to his own life and experience. Millet's work centred on extreme realism and shocked his contemporary society by breaking with the artistic conventions governing subject matter. Gombrich suggests, 'In the academies the idea was still prevalent that dignified paintings must represent dignified personages, and that workers or peasants provided suitable subjects only for *genre* scenes in the tradition of the Dutch masters' (Gombrich 1972: 402). Goldwater and Treves relate how Millet speaks up in his own defence;

Is it impossible to admit that one can have some sort of idea in seeing a man devoted to gaining his bread by the sweat of his brow? Some tell me that I deny the charms of the country. I find much more than charms – I find infinite glories. I see as well as they do the little flowers which Christ said that Solomon, in all his glory, was not arrayed like one of these. I see the halos of dandelions, and the sun, also, which spreads out beyond the world its glory in the clouds. But I see as well, in the plain, the steaming horses at work, and in a rocky place a man, all worn out, whose 'Han!' has been heard since morning, and who tries to straighten himself a moment and breathe. The drama is surrounded by beauty.

It is not my invention. This 'cry of the ground' was heard long ago. My critics are men of taste and education, but I cannot put myself in their shoes, and as I have never seen anything but fields since I was born, I try to say as best I can what I saw and felt when I was at work. Those who want to do better have, I'm sure, full chance.

(Goldwater and Treves 1976: 292–3)

How does this individualistic concern with imagery differ from the intention of crafts-people? One major difference is that the latter are mainly concerned with making a functional artefact. Craftsmanship involves a high level of skill, using techniques and processes drawn from long-established traditions. Carol Hogben of the Victoria and Albert Museum describes the potter Bernard Leach as a craftsman who:

thinks in primal images, and likes to keep his mind on central themes. ... To be a potter and so work with one's hands (using wheel, water, clay and draught-fed fire), while at the same time being also an artist, and kneading out the feeling of one's life, is to him a simply blissfully high calling.

(Hogben 1978: 9)

Hogben suggests that Leach found a balance, using his distinctive but traditional hand-making methods, between creating unique pieces and manufacturing useful but repetitive wares for everyday use. He was a craftsman operating within long-established methods of working and yet managed to create within this tradition his own personal way of making art.

Considering design, what does a designer 'do' when designing? The Keith-Lucas Report of 1980 (Fairbairn 1987) on 'Design Education at Secondary Level' suggests:

 To design is always to provide some form, structure, pattern or arrangement for a proposed thing, system, or event. A design is always an integrated whole, a balanced prescription – a product of judgment and invention as well as skill.

(Fairbairn 1987: 3.3)

The designer's intention may be summarised as a concern with initiating a design and in some cases making an artefact, system or environment that conforms to a specific brief. This brief may be self-generated or be given by somebody else. Craftspeople and designers, in contrast to the artist, often make artefacts that serve a clearly defined functional purpose. However, artists often work to a specified commission, so the distinctions inevitably become blurred.

Looking for similarities

If the criteria above are the distinguishing differences between artists, craftspeople and designers, then which aspects are common? Figure 1.3 describes the overlap in terms of shared media, equipment and processes and the shared concern with aesthetic awareness, appreciation and judgment.

It can be seen from Figure 1.3 that we suggest that aesthetic awareness and an understanding of media and processes is common to all three activities. For example, in

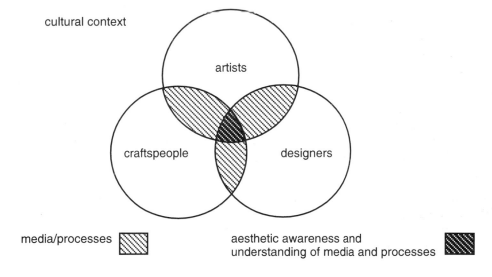

Figure 1.3 Diagram of the interrelationship of art, craft and design

designing a ceramic dish with a decorated surface, the craftsperson will have to take into account the line, pattern, colour and perhaps form of the surface design. In so doing the craftsperson is making decisions about balance, proportion and harmony which underpin aesthetic judgement. These considerations will also be pertinent to the painter who is making a representation on the surface of the canvas. In traditional thinking, aesthetics was defined as the appreciation of the beautiful, but now the term is given a broader meaning to include the many ways in which we may respond to satisfactory arrangements of forms, surfaces, colours, spaces and materials. This may relate to pictures or clothing, furniture or sculpture.

It is important to view art, craft and design as part of a wider cultural context. Our aesthetic understanding and awareness are dependent on what kinds of 'art' we encounter and in what ways we think about such objects.

In units 5 and 6 we return to the distinctions between artistic and aesthetic awareness and development, with particular regard to children's development. In the following teacher activity you are invited to consider the similarities and differences between art, craft and design.

 TEACHER ACTIVITY 1.4

First, read each of the following extracts carefully. Then discuss with a colleague the ways in which you are able to analyse them in terms of their relationship to art, craft and design. It will become apparent that each extract deals with all three, but with a different emphasis in each case. You may find each extract initiates debate and considerable differences of view. You may find it helpful to take each extract in turn and rate it on all three headings in a proportional way, e.g. art 0–10, craft 0–10, design 0–10.

Extract 1

 Sir Joseph Paxton's unique stroke of inspiration [was] the original Crystal Palace for the Great Exhibition of 1851. This superb, if over-familiar, monument represented a major instance of mid-nineteenth century Victorian architecture which reflected the traditions of regularity and simplicity of the architecture of 1880. Simultaneously, it utilises to the full the principles of assemblage and reuse of elements that was made possible by early techniques of mass production. In this respect the Crystal Palace reflects not so much the period in which it was built, but rather an aesthetic point of view that shares elements in common with its immediate past (the first, Romantic Classic phase of modern architecture), and of the future (in the more frankly modernistic architecture of the twentieth century).

(Jacobus 1963: 921)

Extract 2 An interview with Victor Pasmore.

 'In traditional painting you start with the landscape which is simplified down and forced into the geometry of the rectangular picture plane. To some extent the Cubist did that, I thought I'd try the reverse. I start the picture with abstract painting and then try to develop the representation from that.' He sees this as a more independent form with a deliberately stylised linear design working over the top of the paint. 'I had to do it in terms of an idea, it's not done from looking at the thing. I remember criticising a drawing of a cat by one of my grandchildren when she was very small. I said, "That doesn't look much like a cat", and she said, "It's pretence". I thought this was a first-class description of art. At over eighty I thought I'd try the same thing myself – pretence.'

(Lambirth 1993: 49)

Extract 3 A review of Joanna Constantinidis' pots.

Joanna's pots are made in series, and the recent form is no exception. There is a constant desire by her to improve upon the last pot, by way of progression. The present pots are tall thrown pieces made in a white stoneware/T material 50:50 mix. This series was first made in porcelain for its delicacy but the joins and seams were continually visible. The forms are slightly ovaled and a ridge is beaten on one side with her palms to make a flange. An indentation is made down the seam with a tool or a finger and then reinforced with a large coil. This fills up and strengthens the indentation, and is then completely smoothed over. The surface is then scraped with a coarse scraper and then a fine one. Finally, the pot is burnished with the back of a spoon to give a definition and slight texture. A stamp is finally applied as a full stop to that part of the making process.

(Walter 1995: 11)

The discussion has so far focused on teasing out and developing our ideas about the nature of art, craft and design in order to inform our teaching. Now we will consider the views of children.

HOW CHILDREN DEFINE ART, CRAFT AND DESIGN

Teachers are used to checking that the terms they use in their teaching are readily understood by the children. As art, craft and design as distinct categories may be new terms for some children, perhaps it is wise to find out how children understand them. As we write, Christmas has taken over most primary schools. Classrooms, corridors and halls have been transformed by teachers and children into glittering, exciting celebrations of the festive season. Watching some children creating a crib scene we wondered whether their notion of what 'art' was would include such an activity. And if this were the case, would their views about art in any way match the broad definitions above? So we asked a group of children to tell us what 'art' meant to them, and then questioned them further about craft and design.

Susan and Tom are both 10 years old. They were asked what the term 'art' meant to them.

Susan	Painting and drawing.
Tom	Well, when I think of art I think of all sorts of things, I go to the Arts Centre a lot and I know art is not just drawing, art is the arts, I think a lot about music and like Susan said, painting and drawing and embroidery, music recording and that.
Interviewer	Well, if we just stick to the visual arts, not music and drama and poetry but just …
Tom	Well, I think about etching and collage …

The children then related the experience they had making a large-scale collage from natural materials based on the four seasons and explained that the idea had come from a video where they had seen some sculptors making a similar one in a forest. They were then asked what they thought 'craft' implied:

Susan	If you said craft to me the first thing I would think of would probably be knitting because my Nan does a lot of knitting.
Tom	Stitching and making decorative cakes and things …
Susan	I've got a favourite craft and that's quilling. We did faces in clay and I made a pot and at Brownies and we could make anything we liked and I made an egg pot for my little brother.
Tom	Yes, and I made a present for my drum teacher, it was of a drum set.
Interviewer	And what about 'design'?
Susan	There's housing design, my Dad used to do that.
Tom	Jeff Banks is a clothes designer … well, anything has to be designed….

They were then asked to think how art might be considered different from design.

Tom	Well, art I would have thought was more like a reproduction whereas design is actually making a new thing. In art you've got this thought in your head of exactly what it looks like and then you draw it or you copy something or you copy another picture, but whereas in design you draw designs and make a new thing.
Interviewer	Well, an artist might disagree with that and say 'my painting is completely new and nobody else has ever made one like this!'
Tom	That would be a completely different type of painting, maybe … I can't think of anything!
Susan	Like Picasso chose different ways of painting that had never been done before.
Tom	I know, or maybe it's like getting a bit of 'Corroflute' and using one of those burners that you use for burning into wood and you could melt the board to make something.

These children were certainly able to tease out the differences between art, craft and design, perhaps basing their ideas on previous discussions with adults or work done with their teacher on art and artists. It is vital for student teachers and teachers to have a clear view of the differences and similarities of art, craft and design so that they can plan and teach appropriately. It is also important that children have a shared perception of what these terms mean so that they better understand the nature of the tasks set them by their teachers.

The following activity examines the match between teacher and child understanding.

 ## TEACHER ACTIVITY 1.5

Devise some simple strategies to enable children to think more deeply about the differences between art, craft and design. Here are three ideas to start you off.

Key stage 1/2: people who make art

Make some cards, using pictures from magazines and postcards, that show 'people concerned with making' as artists, craftspeople and designers. Use these cards to generate discussion with small groups or the whole class. Refer to these key questions in your discussion with the children.

Key Questions

Art – artists
1   What is this person doing?
2   What object are they making?
3   What materials are being used?
4   What is the object for?
5   What do we get from it?

Craft – craftspeople
1   What is this person doing?
2   What object are they making?
3   What materials are being used?
4   What is the object for?

Design – designers
1   What is this person doing?
2   What is being designed?
3   What materials will be used in making it?
4   What will it be used for?

Key stage 1/2: categorising artefacts

Make up a collection of artefacts that fall clearly into the three categories. These might include a painting, a small sculpture or ornament, a clay pot made by a child, some designed and factory-made objects such as a pair of shoes , a watch and a pen, a hand-knitted garment and a piece of embroidery. Ask the children to sort the artefacts into categories and discuss the way that some artefacts may cross the boundaries between art, craft and design and why this may be so.

Key stage 2: 'Happy Families'

Ask the children to design and make a 'Happy Families' art, craft and design game with families of Mr, Mrs, Master and Miss Painter, Potter, Architect, Sculptor, Weaver, etc. The game would be played in exactly the same way as Happy Families where the object is to collect sets of families. The winner of the game would be the first child to collect a family of artists, a family of craftspeople and a family of designers. The children must justify their categorisation to their peers and their teachers. The intention in playing the game would be to ensure the correct use of the terms art, craft and design and associate them with the varied artists, craftspeople and designers.

SUMMARY

In this unit we have outlined some common ideas and misunderstandings about art. Drawing, painting, sculpture and other art forms have their own traditions, which underpin the art of both past and present. We have suggested that a knowledge of these traditions can inform our understanding of the subject and how we can make artists' work meaningful to ourselves and the children we teach.

In talking about art we have not proposed an elitist view but described how individuals encounter art in their everyday life. We have suggested logical ways of 'reading' a picture, which is informed by a better knowledge of art and art history.

We have discussed the relationship between art, craft and design and pointed out the similarities and differences between them. This has been done to aid clarity in understanding and teaching the subject. Finally, we have placed 'art' within the context of the National Curriculum, providing a framework for understanding both the attainment targets and the relationship between them.

In the next Unit we examine ways in which a knowledge base for the subject can be established. The relationship between current theory and practice in art education is explored, and activities are suggested to encourage teachers to reflect on their own experience in relation to theory. This will help to identify how a knowledge base for art can facilitate teaching.

A knowledge base for the subject

In Unit 1 we opened a discussion about the nature and complexities of art. Its meaning and purposes are subject to continuous reinterpretation according to prevailing opinion in any particular period or cultural tradition. Philosophers, poets, historians, cultural observers, critics and not least artists themselves continue to debate the meaning of art, and its relationship to the artist and the spectator. As educators, we need to look at the notion of children's art in the context of schooling in order to identify a suitable subject knowledge base for teaching art.

The value and significance of children's art was first recognised in the late nineteenth century by Ruskin (1857) and other pioneer thinkers. In the twentieth century these ideas were developed in the work of Lowenfeld and Brittain in 1947, Arnheim (1954) and Kellogg (1969). They contributed to notions of developmental stages in art which, in modified form, underpin the work of present-day educationalists and psychologists. Art education, in terms of children's art being valued and activities being provided in schools, owes a great deal to these early theorists. On the other hand, their work was also responsible for perpetuating the idea that children's art was largely concerned with spontaneous, self-generated, uncritical self-expression.

Obviously, every child's work is based on personal experience but we have come to understand that children's art is not produced in a vacuum. Their work does express their personal, affective response to experience but, importantly, it is now recognised how it also draws on their knowledge and understanding of the well-established artistic traditions that form part of each child's experience. Taylor quotes Oliver Bevan, an art educator who recognises this:

 The teaching of art has two aspects – Janus-like – looking out towards the visual language evolved by the culture we share and looking inwards towards the individual student's expressive needs.

(Taylor 1986: 174)

Teachers are beginning to recognise children's art work as not only self-expressive activities based solely on sensory experience, but also affected by their knowledge of the form and content of the work of established artists – the subject knowledge base for teaching art. Such form and content is also, of course, associated with feeling, but in particular draws on traditions, genres and styles including historical painting, the portrait, the still life, and the landscape. This new interpretation of children's art places it more firmly in the public domain, to be shared by others, rather than perceiving it as lodged only in the 'secret garden' of an individual child's self-expression.

It follows from this that it is necessary for children to know about the work of acknowledged artists in order to enable them to make comparative judgments between their own work and that of other artists. This, in turn, may enable them to produce practical work of increased quality and to share with others ways of viewing the world through artistic traditions. For example, a child's paintings of sunsets may achieve greater depth if they have an understanding of the vision and technique of J.M.W. Turner.

Roger Fry, painter, art historian and influential critic, recognised this 'shared vision' in 1937 when he wrote:

> in our reaction to a work of art there is something more – there is a consciousness of purpose, the consciousness of a peculiar relation of sympathy with the man who made this thing in order to arouse precisely the sensations we experience. And when we come to the higher works of art, where sensations are so arranged that they arouse in us deep emotions, this feeling of a special tie with the man who expressed them becomes very strong. We feel that he has expressed something which was latent in us all the time, but which we never realised, that he has revealed us to ourselves in revealing himself.

(Taylor 1986: 6)

These sentiments, although couched in the language of the past, are central to the thinking which underpins this book:

1   The 'consciousness of purpose' suggests a positive intention on the part of the spectator to engage vigorously with and 'interrogate' the picture.
2   The intentions of the artist are made explicit in his work, in order to arouse precisely the sensations we experience as spectators.
3   When Fry talks of 'higher works of art' his suggestion is that paintings considered to be 'masterpieces' have stood the test of time because they convey messages that transcend the period in which they were painted.
4   The artist and the spectator are bonded with a 'special tie' of emotion and sensation through this recognition of commonality with the artist.

What is probably of most importance to education is the idea that when we actively and purposefully engage with a work of art some of its meaning is transferred to the spectator. This leads the spectator to a more elaborated perception of the physical world, partly conditioned by their experience of viewing the work. Some people may have had the experience of emerging from an art exhibition and finding that their perception of the surroundings has been totally coloured by the pictures they have seen. For a moment they have been viewing the world through the artist's eyes. Works of art have within them the potential to change our view of the world. Through their forms and symbols they elaborate the perceptions of the spectator, and often encapsulate touchstones of human experience.

SELECTING FROM THE KNOWLEDGE BASE

One of the problems of deciding what a knowledge base for art education might embrace is the huge range of practical activities and stimulus materials. These include both first-hand and second-hand experience of art from all times and all cultures, and also the plethora of images accessible on print, film and video. New technologies, such as the Internet and CD-ROM, can now bring to the classroom images from the world's major galleries and museums. How does a primary teacher select the most appropriate of these for the primary classroom?

The idea of 'touchstones of human experience' gives some clue as to what might be appropriate works of art and artistic activity for primary teaching. In speculating about what those touchstones are that link both art and life, the following are likely to be common factors: the relationships between people, especially within the family; our enduring links with nature, manifest in landscape, townscape and seascape painting; the interiors of houses and the objects that surround us; our relationship with the animal kingdom; and, perhaps most important of all, our perception of ourselves, as we feel we are and as we would like to be. Our perception of ourselves would necessarily include a spiritual dimension linking us with the forces of nature and religion.

Later in this Unit we look at the work of Mary Cassatt and Pablo Picasso, and although we will see great contrasts in the style and content of the paintings and the mood that they convey to the spectator, what they share is the touchstone of the relationship between people, nature and the environment.

Children continuously make pictures about what they know and feel. The children's work will share with other artists a concern with the subject but will be less sophisticated. It will often be drawn from direct experience, as in 10-year-old Elizabeth's painting of her dog (Plate 4), which is similar in content and mood to Mary Cassatt's painting (Plate 3).

Some children's art can be a reaction to events filtered through another medium, for example television, and this determines the nature of the work they produce. For the majority of children in our schools their concept of war, for instance, is from secondary sources (books, cartoon strips, film and television), and therefore the drawings by Nicky (aged 6), although action-packed, portray war as a 'game' rather than a human tragedy. The drawings by a Year 6 class (Figure 2.2) show not only their increased drawing ability, but also a more sensitive understanding of what war means. Their work has also been informed by close scrutiny of Picasso's *Guernica* and they have utilised some of the exaggeration and distortion, emphasised by jagged, broken lines, that Picasso employed in his work.

The following teacher activities draw on war as one of the touchstones of human experience, and are designed to help you explore the images in Picasso's painting. In this activity you will consider just how the artist succeeds in engaging your interest and emotion.

Figure 2.1 Nicky: *War*

 TEACHER ACTIVITY 2.1(a)

In discussion with colleagues look at Picasso's painting *Guernica* (Figure 2.3) using the same criteria as in Unit 1:

1   The subject – what do you think the picture is about?
2   What are the main artistic devices the artist has used (e.g. main tonal scheme, brushstrokes, light and shade, composition)?
3   The mood – what is the atmosphere and how does the artist convey this?
4   Your reaction to the picture – how does the picture make you feel?

Consider the painting. It may convey to you a notion of panic and pain. Just how does each part of the painting describe the blast of bombs, the fear of people and horses, the dismemberment of bodies and the scream of pain? Reflect on how the work effectively conveys the combination of the exterior world of the bomber and the interior claustrophobia of bombed buildings and suffering people.

 TEACHER ACTIVITY 2.1(b)

Consider the painting *Guernica* again. Through tracing or free-hand drawing, try to record and imitate Picasso's use of the following formal elements:

*   line – sharp, angled lines rather than curves
*   shape – mostly jagged and angular
*   pattern – plain against patterned areas
*   tone – sharp tonal contrasts, black and white

 TEACHER ACTIVITY 2.1(c)

Continue this analysis by deconstructing the explosive composition of *Guernica*. Lay tracing paper over the picture and sort out the main basic shapes that make up the composition. For example, draw a line to show the major triangle which includes the bottom edge of the picture and rises to a point above the flame, to the

Figure 2.2 Pablo Picasso: *Guernica* © Succession Picasso/DACS 1997

Figure 2.3 Year 6 children: War

right of the horse's head. Continue to explore the main divisions and shapes within the picture so that its structure is exposed.

These activities will have demonstrated the relationship between the content of a painting, its effect on the spectator and how the artist's view is expressed through the formal elements of art. It can also be observed that Picasso's image of war, although complicated, has a powerful and enduring effect on the spectator. Somehow the complexity of the image lasts and penetrates the mind more fully than the children's pictures of similar content. Through this activity you may find that, in Fry's words, Picasso 'has expressed something which was latent in us all the time, but which we never realised, [and] that he has revealed us to ourselves in revealing himself'.

Studying these works by Cassatt, Picasso and the children helps us to understand how a selection from the wide knowledge base might be made. The selection could start in one of three ways:

1   *The subject matter* – which draws on a child's direct or indirect experience, for example playing in the garden with a dog; eating ice cream; a stormy day at the seaside (Plate 5).
2   *Choosing an artist's painting* – looking at an artist's work, which could relate to the child's experience in some way, for example Mary Cassatt's *Woman with Dog* or Renoir's *A dance at the Moulin de la Galette*.
3   *The formal elements of art* – which relate to the content or mood and make the images meaningful, for example Picasso's *Guernica*, or the adventures of Superman, which also employ angular zig-zag lines and maximum contrast of tone and pattern.

These three starting points may enable teachers to compile a selection of images that are most appropriate to their needs, and offer a route into the hinterland of art. They also draw on knowledge, experience (understanding) and skills – identified by those responsible for devising the National Curriculum for Art as the key components of the two attainment targets.

ART AND THE NATIONAL CURRICULUM

Making art is a complicated business, bringing together within the work the artist's knowledge, experience, skill, and their ability to express feeling and to communicate through images.

These matters are dealt with within the National Curriculum, and the Art Working Group's interim report of 1990 provides a useful working analysis of the subject, as far as teaching and learning are concerned:

 art and design is concerned with visual communication, aesthetic sensibility, sensory perception, emotional and intellectual development, physical competence and critical judgement. Its particular contribution is concerned with the observation and recording of visual images, and through them, the expression of feeling and emotion, the transformation of materials into images and objects, the skills of planning and visualisation, the intuitive, as well as the logical, processes of designing, and the study of the work of artist and designers.

(DES 1991: 7)

This quotation encapsulates the complexity of art and design, but does not provide any strategies for planning particular programmes of work or lessons designed to deal with specific issues. However, the two attainment targets for art provide a more digestible description of what is set out above and because they are attainment targets they indicate learning objectives and emphases for planning. More particularly, as stated in the National Curriculum for Art:

> Pupils' understanding and enjoyment of art, craft and design should be developed through activities that bring together requirements from both Investigating and Making, and Knowledge and Understanding wherever possible.

(DES 1991: 2)

In order to understand better how they might be best brought together it is worth considering them separately and then discussing where they might overlap.

Attainment target 1 – investigating and making

Investigating what? Making what? Investigating implies a spirit of enquiry and a search for new knowledge. It might include the interrelationship between media, gathering resources

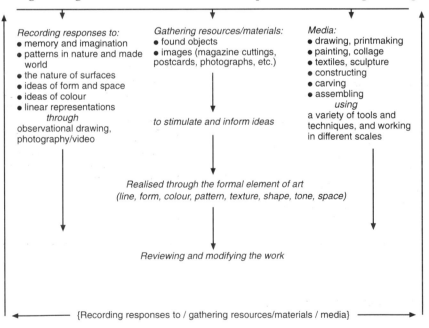

Figure 2.4 Investigating and making

and materials and recording responses to a variety of different stimuli as demonstrated in Figure 2.4.

Attainment target 2 – knowledge and understanding

Knowing what? Understanding what? Knowledge implies an established bank of concepts, ideas, facts and information about art. As we reflect on that knowledge and recognise the importance and relevance of facts and information, we gain greater understanding of the nature of art and its history and processes. Further, the National Curriculum requires children to apply their knowledge and understanding to their own work. Figure 2.5 illustrates the main components of the attainment target, in the form of suggested practice. The components, although separated out for clarity, relate to each other. In each of the boxes the activities enable the learner to acquire more knowledge and reflect on this to gain more understanding of art, its history and processes.

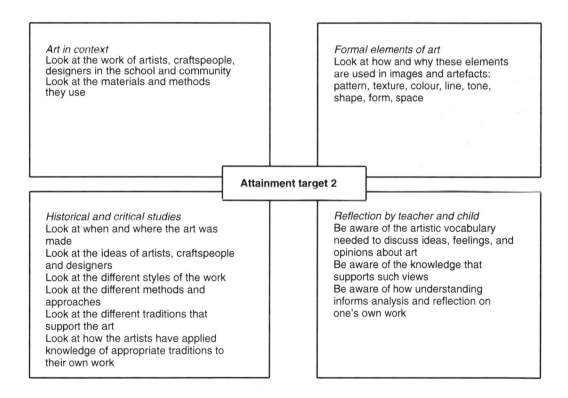

Art in context
Look at the work of artists, craftspeople, designers in the school and community
Look at the materials and methods they use

Formal elements of art
Look at how and why these elements are used in images and artefacts: pattern, texture, colour, line, tone, shape, form, space

Attainment target 2

Historical and critical studies
Look at when and where the art was made
Look at the ideas of artists, craftspeople and designers
Look at the different styles of the work
Look at the different methods and approaches
Look at the different traditions that support the art
Look at how the artists have applied knowledge of appropriate traditions to their own work

Reflection by teacher and child
Be aware of the artistic vocabulary needed to discuss ideas, feelings, and opinions about art
Be aware of the knowledge that supports such views
Be aware of how understanding informs analysis and reflection on one's own work

Figure 2.5 Knowledge and understanding

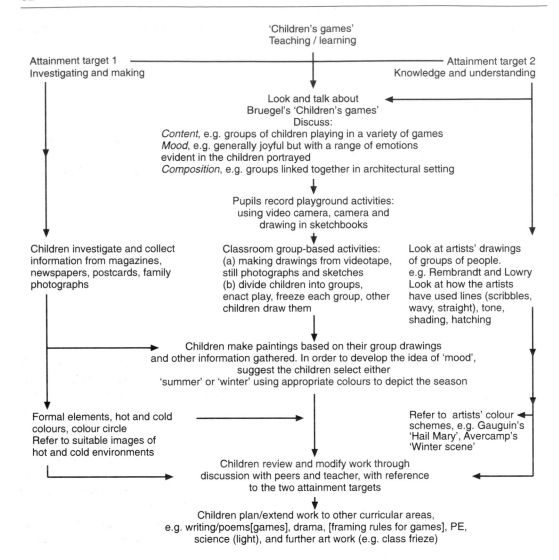

Figure 2.6 Children's games

The interrelationship between the two attainment targets

The interrelationship between these two attainment targets is best illustrated by reference to a particular classroom-based example; this is followed by some activities that will provide practice at devising programmes of work with starting points based on a formal element, an artist's picture, or subject matter. Figure 2.6 outlines such a programme with the starting point of an artist's picture for the children to consider, within an overall theme of 'children's games'.

The following activities are designed to help you appreciate how the two attainment targets might fit together in practice.

TEACHER ACTIVITY 2.2

Plan a short programme (e.g. three lessons) incorporating some of the components from the two attainment targets on the theme of 'journeys'. It would be useful to adopt the planning approaches suggested earlier, i.e. the three starting points of:

1   subject matter
2   choosing an artist's painting
3   the formal elements of art

TEACHER ACTIVITY 2.2(a) (SUBJECT MATTER)

Brainstorm with children the idea of 'A trip away from home', drawing on their actual experiences. From this develop a programme for art which will include aspects of attainment target 1 and attainment target 2. For example, children could be asked to do a drawing or painting about 'leaving home'. Looking at the townscapes of L.S. Lowry or railway station paintings such as Monet's *The Gare St-Lazare* will help the children to make connections between their work and the way other artists use lines, colours, patterns and other compositional devices. The children might discuss similarities and differences in the subject matter between 'then' and 'now', with reference to material such as travel brochures. In addition, the children may discuss the different emphases they might want to make in their subject matter, compared with (adult) artists from a different period or country. This discussion will inform the choices they make about their practical art work.

TEACHER ACTIVITY 2.2(b) (CHOOSING AN ARTIST'S PAINTING)

Introduce children to the painting of an artist who has concentrated on the theme of journeys, e.g. Monet's *The Gare St-Lazare*. Use the questions suggested in teacher activity 1.1 (page 12) to help you plan what you will ask the children in your lessons.

After discussing the painting with the children, talk about the artistic devices used by the artist and about the content and mood of the work. Then plan a series of art lessons, in similar manner to the example of 'Children's games' (page 32), that enable the children to apply their new understanding of the artist's work to their own practical drawing and painting. For example, the children might decide how they will use certain elements of art (such as colour or tone) to achieve a similar mood in their art work.

TEACHER ACTIVTY 2.2(c) (THE FORMAL ELEMENTS OF ART)

Plan a series of lessons that introduce children to line and tone in order to build the children's understanding and practice of these two formal elements. Drawing a bicycle would reflect the theme of journeys and give the children first-hand experience of working from observation (linear spokes, the light and dark of cog wheels, the curved form of the saddle). Support this work (based on attainment target 1) with analysis of how artists convey movement (attainment target 2). Look at Giacomo Balla's *Dynamism of a dog on a leash* and *Speeding auto*, or Umberto Boccioni's drawings of cyclists.

CRITICAL STUDIES

Throughout this Unit it has been assumed that teaching children how to 'make art' is intrinsically related to teaching them about the processes and procedures of working artists. It has also been assumed that an understanding of how art in its various forms is produced in different historical and cultural contexts is necessary to a proper education in the subject. The historical and critical study of these matters, because of its analytical and reflective nature, is what links the learner to the world outside their personal concerns and imagery, and enables them to relate their work to the public domain. It has been argued that this process is beneficial to children's art making, and not a 'bolted-on' addition. Rod Taylor produces a clear and concise summary of this:

Critical studies in art education, then, does not represent a newly invented and separate curriculum area divorced from children's practice of making art and craft objects. It is sometimes an independent activity in which the focus is on the study and contemplation of visual arts objects in their own right, and at other times it involves complex and subtle interrelationships with the children's own work. Once this is accepted, its significance and breadth can be fully appreciated because it can form the basis of an approach to art education in which pupils can experience all the benefits and virtues implicit in making art: development of analytical and observational skills, sustained application, personal expression, etc. But simultane-ously, they can have opportunity to look outwards to the whole diverse world of the visual arts, and to see their endeavours as part of this larger whole with each aspect nurturing, affirming and enriching the other.

(Taylor 1996: 280)

This seems to incorporate the best of those ideals and principles extolled by Fry (1937), Arnheim (1954) and others, as well as the National Curriculum requirements, in a way that is accessible to all and manageable within the primary school context. Establishing a critical studies perspective in the art curriculum will create the desired knowledge base for the subject.

SUMMARY

This Unit has concerned itself with a knowledge base for art in the context of primary education. The importance of children knowing about and relating their own work to certain traditions, through a historical and critical study of art and artists, has been emphasised and strategies have been suggested for selecting appropriate teaching material from the vast range now available to teachers. Furthermore, starting points for this task have been suggested. The National Curriculum for Art has been outlined, including the interrelationship between the two attainment targets. Ways have been suggested whereby teachers may build their knowledge and skills in 'reading pictures' to enable them to plan similar activities for children.

These ideas are further extended in Unit 3 where models for teaching and learning in art are developed.

Unit 3

Models for children's process of learning in art, and teaching strategies to support learning

In this Unit we suggest some models that describe the process of children's learning in art, and the necessary teaching strategies that will support that learning. We continue to stress how important it is for the teacher to understand the particular nature of visual art and its processes so that they can better support children's learning.

Underpinning this Unit is the notion of reflective practice in teaching – a willingness on the part of the teacher to engage in self-appraisal and development (Pollard and Tann 1987). Teacher activity 3.1 draws on Pollard and Tann's work about characteristics of reflective teaching and is designed to challenge your thinking about your own practice, and to direct your reflection towards issues important to art.

 TEACHER ACTIVITY 3.1

This activity may be used as an opportunity for personal reflection on practice, for discussion with a colleague or added to the timetable for staff discussion over an appropriate period of time, led by the art co-ordinator.

1   Key questions about the National Curriculum and art:
(a) In what ways do you think art contributes to the national culture, intellectual debate and (more broadly) the manufacturing industry?
(b) What role do you think your education plays in your response to the above?
(c) What is the value of an understanding of art to the individual, in school and in later life?
(d) To what extent do the current orders for art correspond with your views in respect of the preceding questions?

2   Key questions about reflecting on teaching art:
(a) By what criteria do you decide that your teaching of art is more or less successful?
(b) To what degree do your own likes or dislikes determine what the children do in art and the extent of their success?
(c) To what extent does your familiarity with particular technical processes (e.g. 3-D construction or printmaking) determine what you teach and how children learn?
(d) Are you satisfied that coherence and continuity of art education is addressed within your school? For instance, to what extent is there curriculum coherence between the practices of different teachers in the year groups?

3   Key questions about teaching competence in art:
(a) Have you planned a systematic programme for art for your class, and built into your teaching opportunities for systematic observation of children that will support your evaluation of their learning?
(b) Have you built into your school curriculum management a role of art co-ordinator whose task it is to develop, monitor and support teaching competence in art, including evaluation and assessment? (These competences are identified by the National Curriculum attainment targets for art.)

4   Key questions about judgements of art teaching:
(a) How confident do you feel in making teacher judgements about your teaching and the children's learning in art?
(b) How does recent educational thinking about art and art education inform your views and affect your judgement?

5   Key questions about examining your attitudes towards art:
(a) How open-minded are you in your thinking about art? For instance, do you believe that graffiti or Carl Andre's Tate bricks are art?
(b) How wholehearted are you in challenging your past teaching of art, and how does this compare with what you consider to be your good practice in other curricular subjects?
(c) How hard do you seek ways to improve your current practice, particularly your knowledge of the subject?

6   Key questions about support for reflection on art teaching:
(a) How often do you talk about art to other colleagues on an informal level?
(b) Have you formalised this by building debate about the subject into your school's curriculum planning?
(c) Is there a way for you to learn about art teaching from other colleagues in your school, perhaps by observing other teachers?
(d) Is there a short- or long-term programme for staff development in your school that supports teachers in improving their knowledge of, and practice in, art teaching, perhaps through Inset?

YOUR OWN STARTING POINT

Your thoughts on how teachers teach art and how children learn about it will reflect the way that you, as a person, deal with new experiences. You may be the sort of person who operates in a very logical way, sifting evidence and grafting the new experience on to your previous understanding. Alternatively, you may be the sort of person who initially feels excited or anxious about new experiences, and after this initial emotional reaction begins to assimilate it.

Teachers will have different ways of approaching their teaching of art, depending not only on the task in hand but also on their own personalities and how they 'feel' about the task. It is necessary to try to work out what kind of person and teacher you are, and then to devise programmes of work which correspond to your way of viewing the way children learn and how they should be encouraged to learn. For example, you might ask yourself if your teaching is led by content – for instance, teaching children about the story behind Picasso's *Guernica*. Or is your teaching informed by a particular view of childhood – for instance, do you see the child as an 'empty vessel' to be filled? Is your teaching led by your belief in a method of children's learning, or is it led by measurable outcomes? The views that underpin your thinking will influence the way that you reflect on your own practice. Consequently, any model of children's learning in art will necessarily depend on the nature of the reflective practitioner as well as that which is being taught and to whom.

We support the view of Louis Arnold Reid (1973), that emotional triggers often initiate the learning process. Figures 3.1(a) to 3.1(c) demonstrate how children's learning in art may be initiated, sustained and developed through this 'impulse/feeling-led' process, and also through 'craft-led' and 'technique-led' processes.

ANALYSING CHILDREN'S PROCESS OF ART MAKING

Figures 3.1(a) to 3.1(c) are diagrams of the reflective process of children's art making. They will help you to understand the process of art making as well as the content of an art curriculum. They describe the process in terms of:

- the inception or foundation of an idea/impulse/feeling
- the development of that idea
- the self-reflective evaluation that leads to an extension of the activity

Idea/impulse/feeling-led process

The process may start with the child's idea/impulse/feeling response to a stimulus. This then forms the foundation from which further work can develop and be extended.

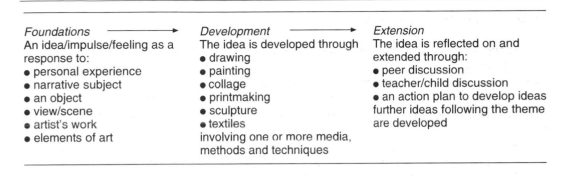

Foundations ————————▶
An idea/impulse/feeling as a response to:
● personal experience
● narrative subject
● an object
● view/scene
● artist's work
● elements of art

Development ————————▶
The idea is developed through
● drawing
● painting
● collage
● printmaking
● sculpture
● textiles
involving one or more media, methods and techniques

Extension
The idea is reflected on and extended through:
● peer discussion
● teacher/child discussion
● an action plan to develop ideas further ideas following the theme are developed

Figure 3.1 (a) Idea/impulse/feeling-led process

Craft-led process

Alternatively the process may start with experiments using a new medium or craft, such as ceramics, textiles or printmaking.

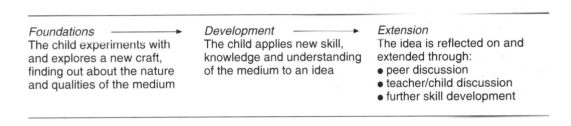

Foundations ————————▶
The child experiments with and explores a new craft, finding out about the nature and qualities of the medium

Development ————————▶
The child applies new skill, knowledge and understanding of the medium to an idea

Extension
The idea is reflected on and extended through:
● peer discussion
● teacher/child discussion
● further skill development

Figure 3.1 (b) Craft-led process

Technique-led process

The process may begin with the child trying out a new technique, for instance drawing with graphite sticks, marbling or taking rubbings from a surface. A specific process is learned, but it is explored in response to a need – finding a way to depict trees in winter, represent the surface of water, or produce texture, for instance.

Foundations ————————▶
The child is introduced to a new method or technique through instruction on the sequential steps of the process

Development ————————▶
The child learns the technique through repeated experiment and experience, matching the technique to their needs

Extension
The child's work is evaluated and extended through:
● peer discussion
● teacher/child discussion
● further experimentation with the technique

Figure 3.1 (c) Technique-led process

It is important to note that the ideas that generate the activities suggested in Figures 3.1(a) to (c) may originate from the children themselves, coming into school fired up about a recent experience and wishing to pursue their ideas in school. Alternatively, ideas may be suggested to the children by the teacher, who chooses a focus as an appropriate starting point for the children's learning. Either way, the idea once initiated sets the process in action.

Also important to note is the fact that talking with the teacher or with peers does not only happen as the work is being extended, but also during the inception and development of the idea. Ideally, it happens all the way through the process, including the point when the child and teacher decide the work is 'finished'. However, it is particularly important for the child to discuss their work with the teacher when the work needs extending. It is often at this point that children, unsupported by adults, lose heart and leave work unfinished or in an unsatisfactory state. It is also at this point that many teachers feel uncertain about their ability to help the child. Later in this Unit we suggest some strategies for teacher intervention that may be helpful.

Although Figures 3.1(a) to (c) represent the learning process as linear, it is better represented as a spiral, which indicates more effectively the continuing, unfolding nature of the experience. We have found a useful parallel in Kemmis's (1982) model of action research and have adapted his model in Figure 3.2 to make this process clear.

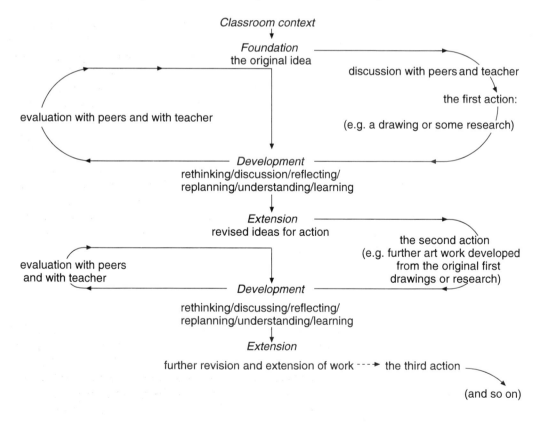

Figure 3.2 The process of children's art making

In parallel to the child's development in the process of art making is a pattern of similar reflective action on the part of the teacher. Pollard and Tann suggest that:

> It is a dynamic process which is intended to lead through successive cycles or through a spiralling process, towards higher quality teaching. This model is simple, comprehensive and certainly could be an extremely powerful influence on practice.

(Pollard and Tann 1987: 12)

THE INFLUENCE OF OUR OWN EXPERIENCE

Our own experience in making art as children or students often underpins our practice. The extract below is a student teacher's reflection on his teaching practice. He is a committed student, serious about his teaching, and has an extensive knowledge of art. His enthusiasm permeates all subjects in the curriculum and he is eager to establish an enabling rather than a prescriptive classroom environment. In this conversation he describes his recent art teaching, defending the children's need to experiment and learn about art materials.

> I really let the children use the materials and dive in. I don't care what the mess is, because in my opinion, I don't really think mess comes into it. Let them make as much as they like as long as they've got *art* in the end. We can always clear it up. If we are going to have this strait-jacket on children – I can remember *that* myself as a child! There was one teacher who was prim and proper and swept up the carpet every two seconds and there was really naff art in that classroom! And I had another teacher who said, 'Dive in! and don't worry about the mess.' Yes, because of my own childhood experiences of being able to 'dive in' I feel *that* is something that is really useful in my teaching and I'm still, in my *own* art, doing it. I get mess everywhere myself but I think its good because then you are actually *into* art, you can really get into it and thus *absorb* it. I wanted the children to have that experience. This would obviously lead to the materials being everywhere and it sounds like I'm wanting chaos but it's not that all because it's fairly controlled. I let the children have their rein but not to the extent that it will hurt or damage anything. It took a lot of confidence to do that, even though it was structured.

TEACHER ACTIVITY 3.2

There are clearly strengths and weaknesses in this student's approach. Assume that you are the student's mentor and consider what might be appropriate advice to enable him to improve his professional practice. Bear in mind that all teachers are different and that his personality is an important factor in influencing his teaching style and approach. In framing your advice, reflect on the qualities apparent in his personality and practice, which may be different to your own, and further, the characteristics he will need to develop to become a professional teacher. You might like to formulate your ideas using the following categories:

1   Relationships with children (ethos, discipline and control, classroom presence, etc.).
2   Teaching skills (subject knowledge, teaching 'craft knowledge', class management skills of planning, organising and resourcing materials and children, evaluating and assessing, etc.).
3   Personal qualities (ethos, commitment, attitude, approach, etc.).

REFLECTIVE EVALUATION AS PART OF THE TEACHING PROCESS

'I can't draw this at all!' or 'It's gone all wrong!' are cries from the heart any primary teacher will recognise. Whenever any of us try to make things, write things or devise programmes of work we have to contend with difficulties that need to be explored through conversation. One of the difficulties with making art as opposed to making a cake or making a bed is to know when the task reaches a satisfactory conclusion.

Painting, drawing or writing is in many ways a continuous process, and the products or artefacts which occur as part of this process are steps or stages along the way. We would suggest that all of an artist's work can be seen as one work in its various stages, each work being part of the whole. In teaching we have a particular problem with finding out from children whether their work is complete, whether the same painting or drawing needs developing further, or whether starting a further drawing or painting would be more appropriate. How can we know? How can the children know, and once we have found out what do we do about it?

Figure 3.3 Getting stuck (*a*) A problem with a painting; (*b*) A problem with a model

A key to this process is being able to conduct a conversation about the art work with the child. Sometimes it is necessary to think of strategies that will enable this conversation to take place in the most fruitful way and lead to some kind of appropriate action to develop the work or bring it to a conclusion. You could try adopting one or more of the following strategies.

TEACHER ACTIVITY 3.3

Devise a painting project based on 'the park'. Discuss with the children what the park might contain – trees, flowers, a lake, and so on. Further, establish the weather conditions and time of year. Ask the children to think of a journey through the park which might be happy, sad, threatening or frightening. As narrative is important you might want to link the art work to a writing project. As the children's work develops note when they get stuck, then employ one or more of the following strategies appropriate to their needs. Evaluate the success of the strategy in the light of the children's progress and their ability to complete the project.

Strategy 1

- Ask the child whether they have achieved what they intended.
- Is the *content or subject* of the work what the child intended to depict? This question may suggest a way forward either to bring the work to a conclusion or develop more work in the same series, as an extension of the original idea.

Strategy 2

- Ask what *atmosphere or mood* they intended their work to have. Discuss whether their picture is happy or sad, disturbing or calming, bright or dull.
- Ask them how well it depicts what they 'feel' about the subject and how successfully that feeling has been conveyed to the spectator.

Strategy 3

- Discuss whether they have used appropriate *formal elements* to achieve their intention.
- Suggest modifications of the colour, tone, line, etc. within the work to achieve the desired result.

Strategy 4

- Discuss the outcomes of the particular *technique* which has been used (e.g. whether the paint has been applied in the 'right' way to achieve particular results – for instance, dots and dabs of paint to suggest sunlight on trees, or watery consistency to emphasise a calm sky).

Strategy 5

- Suggest further *research* to the child in order to develop the work in hand or further work.
- Discuss with the child appropriate works by famous artists and point out the relationship between their work and that of the child. This may be a matter of comparing content; for example, the child painting reflections in water may learn from Monet's water-lily paintings or David Hockney's pictures of swimming-pools. Or again, a child having difficulty in painting the myriad colours in grass may overcome this by looking at Seurat's pointillist technique. A dark mood in a child's painting might be better achieved if he or she studies a Turner storm. Ways of painting figures may be enhanced by looking at the crowd scenes of Lowry.

SUMMARY

Within this Unit we have suggested how different models of art teaching can be enhanced by a reflective approach. Both the teacher and the learner can benefit from this approach. Such self-appraisal and development presents a challenge, and we have therefore stressed the benefits of working collaboratively.

An ability to talk constructively with children and colleagues about art making has been identified as an important vehicle in developing reflective teaching and learning. This is because the qualities and nuances of language most closely relate to the nuances and qualities of visual art. Modelling art education needs a reflective mind and certain ways of lateral thinking, reflective practice and conversation seem to be the most effective ways of working through these developments.

We have emphasised the importance of teachers being aware of how their personality influences their teaching. This applies also to children – primary teachers have always recognised the importance of children's individual development.

In the next Unit we discuss the development discernible in children's art work and will be returning to the subject of communication, which is an important part of this development.

Unit 4

Children and their art

The theoretical aspects of this Unit concentrate on models of child development that look at both children's practical art making and their appreciation of art. The teacher activities centre on key areas of development discernible in children's art work and are designed to help teachers recognise and nurture development. Development in art practice is set firmly alongside the development discernible in other curriculum learning areas.

One of the aims of this Unit is to demystify the notion of child art as being somehow innocent and 'untouchable'. This 'mystification' of children's art originates in the ideas of the early theorists discussed in Unit 2, who saw child art as spontaneous, self-generated, uncritical self-expression. We have suggested that children's art work is not generated in a vacuum; it draws on their own culture and its traditions. This places the art of children firmly in the public domain where it can be shared by others, including their teachers, who have an important role to play in motivating, guiding and supporting development.

Another reason for the mystification of child art is the 'charm factor'. When adults look at the work of children, for example the painting by Elizabeth of *Me and my dog* (Plate 4), we are often charmed by their work. Children's art often contains an enviable amount of immediacy and freshness. Children seem able to capture the essence of experience in a way that can be quite disarming.

We should respect a child's ability to communicate about themselves to us in this way; however, it is not enough for teachers to be impressed. We also need to understand the defining characteristics of art made by children. They demonstrate the ability to make meaningful works which reflect their perception of the external world and the internal world of their imagination, in a way which preserves the authenticity of their art and also brings it into the public domain.

In this Unit we explore why children's art looks the way it does and how teachers, by developing a greater understanding of the intelligent ways children find to express their ideas and feelings, can structure experiences for children in order to facilitate development.

MAKING ART

All children make art on a regular basis, and for some of these children, making art will be the occupation they elect to follow through secondary education into adulthood. In this Unit, ideas are given about how the art of children can be fostered, developed and sustained through the primary years, offering continuity that will ensure progression.

There are many similarities in the way that children and adults work in making art. Drawing is common to both. In the introduction we outlined some of the remarkable features of drawing; here, three case studies describe the characteristics of drawing in detail.

The case studies will help you to recognise the different purposes and strategies employed whilst drawing, by people of different ages and experiences. They will illuminate the similarities and differences in their intentions and planning, the processes they undergo and self-evaluation of the final product.

Joseph

Joseph is 3 years old. Actually, he will tell you that he isn't 3 anymore, he's 3½. Joseph has been drawing regularly since he was a year old, and has moved from his early 'mark-making' to his first representational drawings. He is on the floor, drawing on a large sheet of paper supplied by his mother (who has discovered that if Joseph is not given paper for drawing he will appropriate any paper he judges suitable). Joseph is drawing with a felt-tip pen. He draws an arch on the paper and then carefully joins it up to make an oval shape. 'This is going to be Daddy, I'll show you. He's going to work on the train. This is his eyes.' He draws two smaller circles and then dots the centres to make the pupil. 'Here's his nose and he's got sunburn on it. Here's his mouth and he's smiling, like that.' He draws a curved line across the lower area of the oval.

He then adds some curving scribbles over the top of his oval. 'Daddy's hair, Daddy's hair has got long.' He adds an extra line to the hair, 'My hair has got long, but Mummy cuts mine

Figure 4.1 Joseph: *Mummy and Daddy*

in the garden.' Joseph sits up and looks at the drawing and then leans over and rapidly draws again. 'Here's Mummy. She's got long hair too.' He takes a final glance at the drawing and then leaves it on the floor.

After marvelling at the first representational drawings, parents stick them on the fridge and kitchen walls where they become a background to everyday life, a part of the multitude of visual images that surround us daily. Soon parents are piling armfuls of drawings in the bin, so productive are their children.

Michael

Michael is 7 years old and is making a drawing in school. He is drawing his family and the sunflower that he has grown at home in the garden and, like Joseph, he talks as he draws. James Britton refers to the work of Vygotsky who suggests that talking acts as self-direction by the child, so can be seen as a commentary and a self-monitoring activity.

> It was Vygotsky who, in commenting upon Piaget's ideas, pointed out that a child's first speech derives from conversations he has listened to and takes the form of social interchange as we have seen: and that only later does the speech thus acquired come to be used in a monologue. He stressed the function of monologue, that of assisting activity, organising a child's experience.
>
> (Britton 1980: 59)

Figure 4.2 Michael: *My family and the sunflower*

Michael starts on his drawing of the sunflower. 'I'll show you, this is Daddy. Daddy is tall, but the sunflower is bigger than Daddy, yet.' He draws in the sunflower stalk and the head of the sunflower.

'Mummy is next biggest and she is the same as the sunflower now.' He draws in his mother beside the flower. 'Here's James, he's little and he's down here. Here's me next to the sunflower and I'm smaller than Mummy.' He draws himself squeezed in between the sunflower and his mother. ' I can reach the sunflower if I go on my toes.' He draws one arm by his side in rough proportion to his body and then elongates the arm nearest to the sunflower and extends it until it touches the sunflower petals. 'There, finished.'

This episode gave Michael's teacher insights into his mathematical understanding of relational size, scale and his developing concept of time. She was also able to monitor his communication skills, and to see Michael solving the problem of portraying his memory of a real, important and personal event in two-dimensional form.

Teachers are skilled at evaluating their pupils' progress in English, mathematics and science. They are less confident in their ability to identify and act on the child's learning and progression in art. Perhaps one reason may be that art is not so much part of a 'common currency' as English and mathematics. As adults we continuously make aesthetic judgments about our homes, our clothes and the objects we select to buy. But we are somehow distanced from the designer and artist who conceived these objects in the first place. Most of us are mystified by what adult artists do, but an understanding of the processes they engage in may well help us find similarities with the way children make works of art.

Alan

Consider Alan Richards. He is an artist also engaged in art making through drawing and, like Michael and Joseph, he is making a drawing based on his direct experience. Unlike the children, Alan is not used to talking to others or even having people around whilst he is working, but agreed to be interviewed in his studio.

Alan points out the main items in his first drawing (Figure 4.3(a)), a cliff face and a descent to the shoreline. He relates that it is his intention to produce drawings that will lead in many cases to painting, but must in themselves represent stages in a developing process; a reciprocation between information gathering and new insights. He explains:

 This drawing is of Little Fistral Beach, so all I had to do was to sit there for as long as it took. It is not done with a view to doing a painting, it is done purely as an exercise in looking, visual acuity, the whole business of hand and eye. My attitude is that whatever you do, whether it's figurative, non-figurative or whatever it attaches itself to, the actual discipline of looking and drawing is very, very important. The procedure for this drawing, and others like it, was to go out after breakfast with my sketch book to sit there, perched on a rock, and draw and try to get into a mode of thinking. We don't always know what we think we know; you can reveal something once you've done the drawing. You don't always know while you are doing it but when you finish. After a hard day's drawing you look at what you've done again and it's surprising what you discover, not only about what you've drawn but about your own development pushed towards something else

Figure 4.3 (a) Alan Richards: *Little Fistral Beach*

Figure 4.3 (b) Alan Richards: *Little Fistral Beach*

you might have seen. It's a reflective process after the event and it leads on to another thing, it's not just cocooned in a vacuum. One drawing releases the potential of another possibility. So the next day I did another drawing more or less from the same place [Figure 4.3(b)]. What I did with this one was to follow the stratification of the rocks, because I was then tuned into something else. That's one procedure and one part of the way in which I approach drawing and the other one is to do a drawing for a painting.

It can be seen that Alan's intentions are not always straightforward. Sometimes they are clear cut, but in other instances they relate to a more discursive process. This is well illustrated by Alan, who goes on, 'I can be out drawing with no intention of doing a drawing to turn into a painting and in the process of drawing something switches on and I suddenly have some other kind of idea.'

Alan talks of a great number of artists who have influenced his work, such as Turner, Constable, Cézanne, Seurat, Goya and Delacroix. Literature, poetry, and his early life in a Welsh community have also influenced his art. He is working within an established tradition, acknowledging his debt to other artists, but at the same time breaking new ground in his fresh approach to the subject and his use of the medium. He is determined to make his own ideas explicit in the work. He wants the drawing and painting to 'work', to succeed, to have some original spark of interest for the viewer that will catch and sustain their attention through several different layers of meaning.

This is apparent in two of Alan's paintings. In his picture *Flowers for Seurat* (Plate 6) there are several references to different aspects of art. The viewer can appreciate:

- a colourful and decorative still life partly painted from observation
- a twentieth century style of composition
- a complex colour/tonal system which is not initially apparent
- through further investigation or specialist knowledge, the viewer will recognise that the use of colour relates to the palette and theories of the nineteenth century painter Seurat.

These layers interact and enable the viewer to appreciate the subtleties of the work and, like the artist, link their sensations and appreciation to their experience and understanding of art. Alan's second painting, the large still life (Plate 7), is based on his first-hand drawing of the landscape of the Exe Valley, Delacroix's *Still life with hare* (1826) and in the foreground, objects gathered from local traders in Exeter who are neighbours and friends of the artist. In this painting he blends the past with the present, his own view tempered by a nineteenth century view. He makes reference to the River Exe as it journeys to the sea and includes artefacts which symbolise the lives of the artist's contemporaries and the nature of his local community. The form and style of the painting represent a unique synthesis of all these components, bringing together observation, memory, imagination and historical knowledge in an original work. This multi-layered aspect of Alan's work will be returned to in Unit 6.

Finding out about how artists of all ages make art is one way for student teachers and teachers to become more aware, not only of the process of making but also (importantly) of the intentions of the maker. This is important because intention is the key motivation for making art, whether you are 3 years old or 53. The procedures, materials and processes involved in the work of art support and give voice to the intentions and express them in some symbolic way. Both Joseph and Michael had intentions in making their drawings, intentions expressed simply but clearly, ' This is going to be Daddy. I'll show you.' Alan, an articulate adult, draws on a language specifically created by art makers to describe the art making process when he talks, for instance, about line, form and shape. However, Alan, Joseph and Michael ultimately rely on the work succeeding, in being able to symbolise both what they think and feel and to communicate that to others.

In describing these examples it is suggested that active, focused observation of people making and talking about art may provide an important starting point for learning about the practice and theory of art teaching. Opportunity for focused observation is very likely to occur during children's art making, teachers' art making, and looking at the work of professional artists. Observing children in your own classroom is the logical starting point. Before that, however, it is advisable to look at some models of children's development in art in order to clarify what you might see and enable you to make some judgments about what teaching is required of you.

MODELS OF DEVELOPMENT IN CHILDREN'S ART

In describing his drawing of Little Fistral Beach, Alan explained how the work developed and how, gradually, the idea or meaning of the work became clear. Willig places the construction and understanding of meaning at the core of art education.

 At its core, art education, in common with all other curriculum areas, is about constructing and understanding meanings. Through the medium of visual symbols, the activity of art enables children to heighten their awareness of, and to express their thoughts and feelings about, people, objects and events of significance in their lives. At the same time, from a teacher's perspective, children's art offers another glimpse of their conceptions of the world, expressed not in language but in visual form.

(Willig 1990: 139)

LOWENFELD AND BRITTAIN'S STAGES OF DEVELOPMENT

How do children develop the visual symbols that Willig refers to above? Studies on this subject by Arnheim (1954), Kellogg (1969), Booth (1977), Goodnow (1977), and Lowenfeld and Brittain (1987) are increasingly well known and offer a reasonable framework on which to build an understanding of development. The work by Lowenfeld and Brittain (1987) will be used as a model in this book, with additional references to appropriate studies. It should be noted that Lowenfeld viewed children's art as an essential creative part of the development of the whole child, and this we would not dispute. He also described this development as the natural growth of the child and felt that influences from adults might have an inhibiting influence on that natural growth. We have made it clear that we feel there is a more prominent role for the teacher than simply being a provider of materials and physical conditions. In this Unit we discuss strategies for teacher intervention that take into account the fact that all children develop at their own individual rate, and that the children in your classes will have different social and cultural influences that will necessarily affect the way their work looks. Their subject matter may be radically or subtly different from the examples we provide to illustrate Lowenfeld's stages, because the work we have used is from mainly from Devon schoolchildren. The social context in which the children in your classes live should have vital impact on their work in the form of influence from their friends, parents, their outside school interests and, hopefully, their teachers!

Another concern we have with Lowenfeld's stages is the fact that he places chronological ages on his suggested stages. From our experience we have found that children we have taught conform only roughly to these ages and we therefore suggest that the stages are best considered without undue reference to the ages. This matter will be discussed more fully as the stages are outlined.

Bearing these reservations in mind, we nevertheless feel that Lowenfeld's model is simple and apt, giving teachers a skeleton framework for reference that will inform their observations of the children's work. Further, it is generally acknowledged by researchers that children from diverse cultures and societies utilise a similar range of strategies in their drawing. Lowenfeld's work offers a useful model to teachers wherever they may be teaching. A key benefit to be gained from an understanding of this model is a new perspective on how to set work for children that will most sensitively match their development.

The following description has been adapted from Lowenfeld and Brittain (1987).

The scribbling stage (age 2 to 4 years)

This stage is illustrated by Figures 4.4 and 4.5. It is characterised by:

- random marks
- child looks away whilst drawing
- action involves whole arm
- marks represent events and passages of *movement* through space and time
- 'action representations' (Matthews 1987) – 'stabbing, banging, slapping'

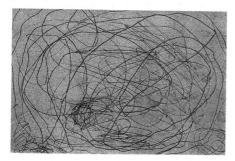

Figure 4.4 Joseph: *Scribbling drawing*

Figure 4.5 Lorna: *Scribbling painting*

John Matthews suggests that children's early symbols are embedded in their early behaviours and physical actions. Drawings can be used by the child to express the actions:

 The child's discovery and use of these structures signals the beginning of understandings which are logical – mathematical, spatial, musical, linguistic and configurative. Embedded initially in the organisation of the child's actions, they are nevertheless the beginnings of symbol and sign usage. These patterns of actions become interiorized to form internal descriptions of reality.

(Matthews 1987: 163)

Matthews suggests that a child needs an environment which 'supports and confirms the validity of his or her early representation'. Some of you may find children's early mark-making ambiguous but Matthews suggests that it is necessary for that to be the case, as the ambiguity has within it the flexibility needed to develop a whole range of symbolic formations with their attendant meanings.

The pre-schematic stage (4 to 7 years)

This stage is illustrated in Figures 4.6 to 4.8. It is characterised by the emergence of certain repeated shapes which stand for something; they represent form. At this stage:

- child names object
- child modifies and refines shapes
- placement and size of objects is determined subjectively according to importance
- child rotates paper when drawing
- oval is often used to symbolise object
- objects are placed randomly
- more detail of body parts
- exaggerated proportion

Paul is older than the other children and his drawing (Figure 4.9) shows more detail. It is interesting to note how Paul has drawn the right leg and then redrawn it larger so that it can reach the ball he intends the figure to be seen kicking! Children at this and the following stage often use this strategy to fulfil an intention, as did Michael in his drawing of the sunflower.

The teacher's role is often one of appreciative adult who, by talking to the child, learns about the subject matter and the important drawing strategies employed by the child. In our experience, the more teachers observe children at any stage, the more respect they have for the ingenuity and logical nature of children's decision making in drawing. It also helps to dispel the notion that children's development should be seen as a deficiency model with children working towards a 'perfect' adult goal in their art work. Continued observation of children at work will illustrate how they invent rule systems that they share with each other and that demonstrate their internal representation of reality in order to portray form, action, and spatial elements.

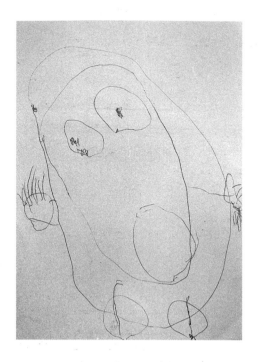

Figure 4.6 Joseph: *A ghost*   *Figure 4.7* Joe: *My family barbecue*

Figure 4.8 Joseph: *Me in the garden with the roses*

The schematic stage (7 to 9 years)

Illustrated by Figure 4.10(a) to (d), this is the stage at which the child develops schemas that describe form. Typically:

- child arrives at fairly definite form concepts in which the 'schema' or form concept is regularly repeated
- there is close attention to detail
- exaggeration and distortion is evident
- enjoyment of pattern
- base line appears
- x-ray drawing
- simultaneous representation of plan and elevation

A wise teacher will capitalise on the child's interest in pattern and detail by selecting activities that help the child to explore objects minutely. Talking to children about why they draw in the way they do will give further

Figure 4.9 Paul: *A big fight is going on*

insights. Jonathan, a 7-year-old boy, when asked why he always drew a line for the ground, commented:

> I'm drawing the line for the ground because it's there. I know I could walk all round the world on the ground, apart from the sea bits, and I'd come back here again, but I just draw it to show it's there. Same as I draw the blue line for the sky. I know the sky isn't starting at a line because I could go up in the air in an air balloon or into space where there's no air but I just draw it like that to show it.

In Victoria's first drawing, Figure 4.10(a), the base of the paper provides a base line for the grass, and the lines at the top of the paper define the sky. This drawing also shows Victoria grappling with spatial concepts, evident in her use of overlapping. She has drawn a tree behind her figure, and behind the dress is a house in the distance, placed on the same base line as the figure.

Jenny's intention in her drawing (Figure 4.11) is to show her walk to school, so the drawing is operating as a map. Her house is at the top left edge and as she draws she explains:

> I come out the door, down the path round the little corner and down the hill. Then I goes up a hill and along the road past the shop and then I stops! *[draws a green asterisk]* 'Cos here's the road I cross with Mrs Baines the lollipop lady. *[She turns the page sideways to draw the road.]* She's stopping the cars so I gets past. And then I goes along a bit and round to school.

In her drawing, the line for the route becomes the base line and objects like the house and tree stand at right angles, on or near the base line. When she gets to the road she changes

Figure 4.10 Victoria: *Ladies*

Plate 1 Auguste Renoir: *A dance at the 'Moulin de la Galette'* (1876). Museé D'Orsay, Paris.

Plate 2 Théodore Géricault (1791-1824): *The raft of the Medusa*. Museé du Louvre, Paris.

Plate 3 Mary Cassatt: *Susan on a balcony holding a dog* (1880). Oil on canvas, 39½ × 25½. In the collection of the Corcoran Gallery of Art, museum purchase, gallery funds.

Plate 4 Elizabeth: *Me and my dog*

Plate 5 A stormy day at the seaside

Plate 6 Alan Richards: *Flowers for Seurat*

Plate 7 Alan Richards: *Still life*

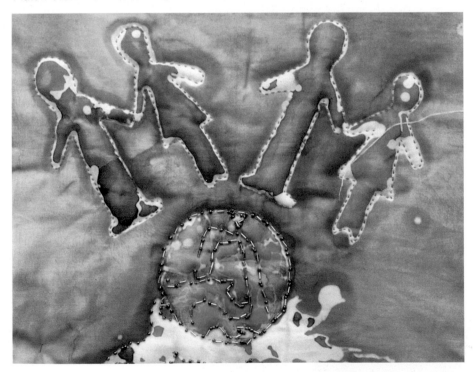

Plate 8 The family – batik and quilting

Plate 9 Alan Richards: *The onset of winter 1 – sowing and planting*

Plate10 Alan Richards: *The onset of winter 2 – after the reaping*

Plate 11 A painting inspired by Picasso's work

Plate 12 Mosaic patterns

Plate 13 Appreciating the richness of textiles

Plate 14 Textiles from around the world

Plate 15 Display representing stimulus, resources and a celebration of the children's work

Plate 16 Children have designed and made masks exploring the new medium of papier maché

Figure 4.11 Jenny: *How I get to school*

the base line to a dotted line on which the cars can then be placed. This is a good example of a child utilising logical strategies to show her growing understanding of spatial relationships. It is also a good example of a child's drawing that might look odd to adults who, unless they had been privy to the conversation with Jen, might have missed the fact that her base line marks the route of her physical actions.

In Figure 4.12 Saeed wants to show his friend his house and is quite happy to show the outside of his home as well as the inside parts. It is an economical and practical strategy to fulfil his intentions. Victoria B (Figure 4.13) is working out on paper a way to show the shape of the round table and her experience of having to surround it with chairs ready for lunch.

She has used the top elevation for the table and side views of the chairs as a shorthand to explain the crowded scene. Both these children were well able to explain their strategies to an interested adult.

Once again, the role of the teacher can be seen as that of a respectful observer who, as a result of the observations, sets children activities that challenge them to explore and expand on a variety of strategies. Suggestions for such activities are developed in Units 5 and 6 alongside other suggestions for teachers to support children's development.

The gang stage (9 to 12 years)

This is the stage of 'dawning realism'. Typically there is:

- self-consciousness about work
- increased awareness of their environment
- understanding of how to represent a 3-D object in two dimensions
- depth conveyed in various ways
- experimentation with learned conventions (perspective)
- greater realism
- disappearance of base line
- overlapping of objects
- less distortion and exaggeration

Figure 4.14 shows Louise's drawing about the effects of war. Louise is striving to show three dimensions in her drawing of the house in the centre of this picture. The base line has

Figure 4.12 Saeed: *My house*

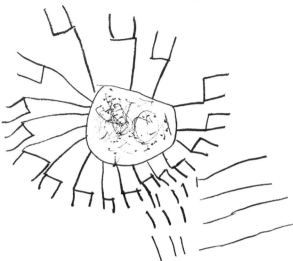

Figure 4.13 Victoria B: *We put the chairs round the table*

been replaced by an expanse of detailed foreground. The horizon is shown by a line that extends behind the buildings, rising and falling, which gives a sense of distance and space to her work.

It should be noted that Louise often shows greater development in her drawing of the figure than in this drawing. In this picture her figures are not the sole centre of interest, but a part of the scene. Consequently, her figures are less developed than if she was drawing a figure from observation. This should not be seen as the child 'regressing' but as a decision to give emphasis to other factors. In this case she has concentrated on showing the destruction resulting from the action described by the explosion of marks that illustrate bomb impact, fire bursting from the church, and the zig-zagging lightning in the sky.

The role of the teacher at this stage continues to be that of interested observer willing to give constructive criticism, as well as that of provider of activities that challenge the children to explore and extend their repertoire of marks and images. Again, strategies for developing and supporting children at this stage will be covered in depth in Unit 6.

How, then, can you as a classroom teacher deepen your observation of children making art? The following activity is designed to give you the opportunity to analyse Louise's drawing, relating your observations to Lowenfeld's work.

Figure 4.14 Louise: *War*

  TEACHER ACTIVITY 4.1

With a colleague, look carefully at Louise's drawing (Figures 4.14 and 4.15). Take time to examine the detail and try to identify what point of view underpins the child's drawing; for instance, does she seem to be interested primarily in the detail of military hardware, or with other aspects of war?

Although her figures are simply drawn, their activity describes the consequences of war on a community. Identify the small details in the drawing that show this. What overall feeling or mood does the work convey? We will not know from where Louise draws her rich knowledge of war unless we talk to her; but where do you think some of this information has come from?

Think about the various ways the child has used drawing marks and devices to show what is happening in the picture, for instance people, houses, explosions. How has the style of the marks been used to convey feeling, a mood, or particular incidents within the picture?

The quiet reflection on a child's drawing required by this activity should have enabled you to learn a great deal about this child's strategies for conveying intentions and meaning. Think how much richer this activity would have been if you had known Louise and taught her daily.

Figure 4.15 Louise: *War* (details)

In the following activity you can draw on the deep knowledge and understanding you have of the pupils in your own class.

 TEACHER ACTIVITY 4.2

Organise your class workload so that the majority of the class are occupied with worthwhile activities whilst you sit with a small group of children who are engaged in a drawing activity. Ask these children to draw something relevant to your class topic or theme that challenges them to find a way of conveying a particular set of emotions or actions. One example might be a link between art and science, a variation on the commonly used exercise of children placing sticks in the earth to monitor the movement of its shadow throughout the day.

The topic might be 'light and shadow' – the relationship of the earth to the sun at different times of the day, and particularly the effect of the sun's rays in creating shadows.

Divide the children into three groups and ask them to draw pictures of themselves playing in a street, riding bikes, skipping, and so on, at the bottom of a hill, with the sun shining and casting their shadows on the ground. The first group should draw pictures of early morning, the second group midday and the third group late afternoon. Discuss with the children how the shadows might appear on the ground and why this might be so.

This activity will help you to ascertain the children's understanding of a scientific concept, but for our purposes it should also allow you to learn more about their ways of drawing. Your role is to observe, and in your observation be aware, first, of how the children deal with the challenge of placing themselves in a street. How do they convey the spaces in the street? How do they show the relationship of the street with the hill? How do they show the houses or shops in the street? Have they attempted to show the three-dimensional form of the houses? How do they deal with drawing the shadows attached to their bodies? Ask the children themselves questions about their drawing strategies.

Collect the drawings and spend some time reflecting on the discernible features as they relate to Lowenfeld's stages of development. The children may be of similar age, but do their drawings all fall neatly into one stage, or are there a range of stages apparent? Did any of the children seem to be having problems in their drawing? Can you see a role for yourself in suggesting follow-up activities to support them in fulfilling their intentions? For instance, do they need some exercises in pencil control, or hatching and shading? Could you support them by setting up a classroom demonstration to show how light and shade affects the way objects look in directional light? Do they need additional information, from photographs or from other artists' work, in order to make their drawings more powerful?

The final teacher activity offers you the opportunity to answer some of these questions in relation to more drawings made by the children in your class.

 TEACHER ACTIVITY 4.3

This activity is designed to highlight the similarities and differences between individual children's drawings. Again your role is of observer, moving amongst the children as they work on their drawings.

Ask all the children in your class to draw a picture using felt-tips on A3 paper, of *one* of the following subjects:

* running up a hill to the top
* we all sat in a circle and ate our ice-creams
* our class doing PE in the hall

All are designed with a view to children drawing figures in a context that will challenge them to adapt or modify their usual schemas. Give the children as long as they need to complete the drawings.

Collect in the drawings and give yourself time to look carefully at the children's work. The following questions may help to focus your reflections:

1   Is there a range of 'stages', in Lowenfeld's terms, evident in the work? Divide the work up loosely into the stages. You know the children in your class well; does the way the drawings divide up have any bearing on the children's general development or are there surprises? For instance, as we have suggested, for some children drawing is the prime means of communication and their drawings will tell you more about them than a conversation or a piece of written English. Conversely, other children much prefer written communication and you may find their drawings less informative than a piece of writing about the same topic.

2   Have the children all utilised similar strategies for describing spatial elements? For instance, have most children utilised a base line or have some indicated the space by using a plan elevation, as in Victoria B's 'top view' of the table?

3   In their drawing of the figures, have the children drawn simply, as Louise did in her drawing about war, or spent time on detailing their figures?

4   How have the children conveyed movement in their figures? Do some of their strategies look 'odd' to you in terms of exaggeration or distortion? If so, can you suggest reasons for the children drawing their figures in this way? Remember our suggestion that its not because the child 'can't draw correctly' but that the child's intention often dictates a specific, purposeful distortion (such as Michael extending the arm in his drawing so that it can reach the sunflower).

This part of the Unit has given you the opportunity to observe children making art and to think about their development. In the next part we look at a theory of development that is concerned with appreciating art rather than making it.

APPRECIATING ART

In this section we are using Michael Parsons' (1987) work on the development of understanding of visual art; that is, aesthetic response. Parsons suggests five stages in this development, that follow each other sequentially from early years to adult life. Parsons assumes, rightly in our view, that 'there must be something serious in art to be understood'. He believes that 'art deals with meanings that are *sui generis* and are not reducible to other kinds of meanings' (xi). He argues that we should look at works of art not just as objects but as aesthetic objects, and base our efforts to understand them on that premise.

How does Parsons believe we come to understand art? In teasing out what it is that people want to understand in art, Parsons identifies certain 'ideas' that he claims are commonly uppermost in our minds when we look at art. He suggests:

 One way to understand how people think is to look at the ideas they use. For example, in thinking about a painting they may consider its subject matter, or its texture and form, or its emotional expressiveness. These are ordinary ideas about what is worth noticing, what makes a painting worthwhile. They are ideas of the sort that ordinary people use. And because they are not very clear ideas they are also ideas of the sort that philosophers of art discuss. From the present point of view, they are important because they structure our thinking about paintings, and, therefore, guide our perceptions and shape our responses. We can understand better how a person thinks about paintings if we know which of these ideas they use and how they understand them.

(Parsons 1987: 14)

Parsons structures the development of these ideas into five stages, but does not tie ages strictly to them. However, he suggests that virtually all preschool children use stage 1 ideas; most primary-aged children use stage 2 ideas; many adolescents use stage 3 ideas; and after that, influences and experience account for the use of stage 4 and stage 5 ideas. Parsons suggests that 'each stage is shaped by a central new insight, and this insight centres in each case on a different topic' (16). This is explained in Figure 4.16.

Parsons suggests that at 'each stage [the child] understands paintings more adequately than the previous one. Each achieves a new insight and uses it to interpret paintings more completely than before' (Parsons 1987: 20).

Stage 1

- The stage characterised by 'favouritism' (what appeals to most children at the time).
- Children show little awareness of the point of view of others.
- Aesthetically, paintings are seen as a stimulus to pleasant experience.

Topics	subject matter	expression	medium, form, style	judgement
[stage 1]	(..............................	favouritism	..............................)	
stage 2	XX	x	x	x
stage 3	x	XX	x	x
stage 4		x	XX	x
stage 5				XX

Figure 4.16 Parsons' stages showing developmental insights at each stage. The large crosses represent the dominant idea or topic

Stage 2

- The subject is the dominant idea.
- There is a belief that the basic purpose of a painting is to represent something.
- A painting is considered 'better' if it is attractive and realistic.
- Skill, patience and care are considered admirable.
- Beauty, realism and skill are objective grounds for judgements.
- Children are able to acknowledge the point of view of others.

Stage 3

- Expressiveness is the idea which marks this stage:

> Intensity and interest guarantee that experience is genuine, i.e. really felt. The feeling or thought expressed may be the artist's or the viewer's, or both. It is always what is inwardly grasped by an individual person.
>
> (Parsons 1987: 23)

- Beauty of the subject matter, the realism of the style and the skill level are all seen as a means to express something.
- There is an awareness that the beauty of the subject matter, the realism of the work or the skill of the maker, are irrelevant when it comes to making aesthetic judgements.
- Creativity, originality, depth of feeling are newly appreciated.
- Responses/judgements are felt to be based on personal subjective experience.
- There is a growing ability to appreciate what Parsons calls the 'interiority of the experience of others' and to grasp and engage with the thoughts and feelings of others.
- There is an ability to appreciate expressive qualities that in the previous stage were judged to be ugly and distasteful.

Stage 4

- A painting is recognised as a social rather than an individual achievement.
- The style and form of paintings are recognised as deriving from existing traditions.
- Art is acknowledged to be in the public domain.
- Objective, criterion-based judgements can be made about art.

> It places the emphasis on the way the medium itself is handled, on texture, colour, form, space, because these are what are publicly there to see; and on style and stylistic relations, because these are how a work relates to the tradition. What is expressed in art is reinterpreted in terms of form and style, and is a public idea rather than a private state of mind.
>
> (Parsons 1987: 24)

It can be seen that Stage 4 is important in terms of our ability to take on several interpretations of a work of art and let them inform our considered judgements. Aesthetically, we are able to find significance in the elements of art, the medium, form and style in order to appreciate what is achieved in the work itself. As Parsons suggests, 'It enables one to find art criticism useful as a guide to perception and to see aesthetic judgment as reasonable and capable of objectivity' (Parsons 1987: 24).

Stage 5

- There is a realisation that concepts and values within traditions constructs the meanings of works of art.
- There is a realisation that values continually change with time, and that judgements are fundamentally both more social and more personal.
- Dialogue with others about thoughts, views and values of art is seen as a way of raising questions rather than transmitting truths.

At Stage 5 one is able to make more subtle responses through a constant re-examination of the practice of art, the reciprocal relationship between the person and the art and the changing values that inform personal response.

Our response to Parsons' stages of development

We feel that Parsons' work represents a very useful model through which children's appreciation of works of art can be viewed. Whilst recognising the usefulness of his work, we would comment that it does not sufficiently take into account the effects of active teaching and learning. The National Curriculum encourages teachers to integrate understanding and appreciation of art with personal research and making. Keeping this in mind, we would maintain that a substantial part of Parsons' developmental sequence can be achieved by children as a direct result of active teaching. Our experience tells us that some children are clearly in Stage 4 at the end of the primary phase of schooling, whilst some adults who have not had the benefit of informed teaching may well be operating in Stages 1 and 2.

SUMMARY

This Unit has explored the development discernible in children's drawing and painting and suggested ways to apply that understanding to the work of children in your school. Reflection on Lowenfeld's stages may have provided you with a new understanding of the ways in which children draw which in turn will help you in your planning and teaching. Obviously, there is much more to children's art than painting and drawing; for example, we have not dealt with their development in three-dimensional work, although the stages outlined here are broadly comparable. Three-dimensional work will be further addressed in Unit 6.

The National Curriculum for Art requires you to teach children to 'read' and understand works of art in their historical context. Parsons' model demonstrates how this can develop in a sequential manner, and in Unit 6 we shall return to this development in respect of lesson planning. Consequently, we have not included in this Unit teacher or pupil activities which relate to Parsons' work.

In the next Unit we will suggest ways in which you can plan programmes of work and those issues which have been discussed so far, whilst taking into account the individual nature of your school.

Planning a programme – principles and practice

It could be assumed in these days of the National Curriculum that planning a programme of work could conform to some nationally agreed pattern and that all schools would construct a curriculum in which the organisational requirements were very similar. However, in our view this does not seem to be the case; our experience suggests that a range of patterns exists according to the characteristics of individual schools. Each school has a different ethos and different way of organising the curriculum.

The National Curriculum, after the Dearing modifications, has been generalised, perhaps to accommodate the diversity within schools. Although this might be welcome, in the case of art much of the previous content (non-statuatory guidance and advice on assessment) has been removed. It could be argued that in these circumstances the document is less useful for teachers engaged in planning, teaching and evaluating the school's programme for art. This book is an attempt to assist teachers in this task and the object of this Unit is to offer some strategies and suggestions for planning a programme. However, these should be adapted to suit the individual needs of your school.

SCHOOLS' OBJECTIVES FOR DEVELOPMENT

All schools now have to set realistic objectives in their long-term planning in which they consider the curriculum that their school is providing. For some schools, planning an art curriculum is a fairly new venture and not all primary schools will have an art specialist on their staff. Usually one member of the staff agrees to take on the responsibility for developing art in the school curriculum.

It would seem to us essential for the school to have a stance on art that is made explicit in a written rationale or school policy, and writing this is often the starting point for an art co-ordinator. This is sometimes a difficult task for a non-specialist teacher to do and it is hoped that the activities in the book so far will provide some insight into the issues to be addressed. Because of the diversity in the needs, requirements, staffing and resourcing of different schools, let alone different teaching and learning styles, no one rationale will possibly serve all situations. A rationale has to reflect the individual nature of your school and be embedded in its procedures.

For those readers whose task it is to write such a school policy the following teacher activity should provide some support. In this activity you are asked to consider a student teacher's rationale for teaching art. It has been composed as part of her training to become an art curriculum leader or art specialist. It reflects the opinions of the writer and is not embedded in the requirements of a particular school. Consequently, it may not be wholly appropriate for your needs but might serve as a starting point for your deliberations. The student teacher was asked to write a rationale, imagining that it would be included in the school's curriculum policy document and that it would be read by other teachers, parents and governors. She was asked to identify the particular characteristics of learning in art and the consequent benefit to children.

TEACHER ACTIVITY 5.1

Read and consider Caroline's rationale (below). Critically analyse its salient features by listing important characteristics under the following headings:

- features unique to art
- ethos and values of the subject within the school
- children – their learning and their school and wider community
- curriculum content and structure

As an experienced and reflective teacher you may not agree with all that the student says.

Construct a rationale for your own school, bearing in mind the criteria above. Remember that this should not exceed 300 to 400 words, as most curriculum documents have to incorporate the ten subjects! Consult with your colleagues when you have made your draft statement and make any amendments suggested. Remember that this statement will need to be revised on a regular basis in order for it to reflect any changes in government or school policy.

Caroline's rationale

The study of art within the curriculum is a crucial part of every child's education. Art speaks, through the formal elements of colour, line, shape, pattern, texture, tone, a universal language that comments on experiences common to all. For this reason, developing the skills to understand and use this 'universal language' is a valuable tool to provide a common ground between all children, regardless of ability, social or cultural background. Therefore the study of art from a variety of different cultures is essential for children to understand how their culture, and that of other people, works, thus reducing prejudice and increasing tolerance.

The skills involved in making different kinds of art can develop hand-to-eye co-ordination as well as heighten sensitive observation of the world around us. Children can use these skills as a form of self-expression, leading to self-awareness, whilst developing other social skills such as communication. Additionally, therefore, through learning about and making art we must provide children with the opportunity to engage with their own experiences, emotions and ideas about art. Therefore, the study of art can be used as a link to other curriculum areas and a way into personal exploration.

To put the study of their own art into perspective, children should be able to respond to works of art independently. The development of critical and analytical skills within the child towards their own work, that of their peers and artists from different periods, cannot be emphasised enough. These are prized skills for any developing child to foster and carry through to adulthood. Not only will they inspire confidence in verbalising personal opinion in other subjects but they will also illustrate the nature of art, that it is open to discussion, that every opinion is valid. Children will also have experience of discussing abstract ideas and concepts, which, in turn, can inform their own work.

Knowledge and understanding of art and artists, including techniques and traditions used, can inform the children's own work. Children must be encouraged to work through the process of art making, with the above in mind, so that they can feel a strong sense of progression and ownership of their work. Originality and imagination must be recognised and celebrated through some kind of exhibition and feedback. A sense of individuality is important to the art-making process but the desire to share and talk about art must be encouraged. This can be done throughout the process, as part of the formative assessment, and at the end go some way towards a summative assessment.

ACTION PLAN

Having sorted out the aims of an art programme by incorporating them within a rationale, the next task is to turn these aims into an action plan that will enable your ideas to be carried out in the classroom. At the beginning of this Unit we discussed the diversity of practice within schools and consequently you will have had in mind how your school's ethos and practice operates when you devised the rationale. The practical procedures of your school will have affected the way in which you constructed your rationale, although they will not have been made explicit at this stage.

The rationale you have devised will form part of the school's development plan for art in the curriculum, which in turn will determine planning, co-ordination of resources, communication within and outside the school, self-monitoring, reflection and future developments.

Action plan: planning

Planning for individual school initiatives in art can be placed alongside general school developments. This in turn will enable senior staff and governors to have a framework within which they can implement their differing responsibilities towards the curriculum and, importantly, make budgetary decisions about resources. This is particularly important for art because of the expenditure involved in consumable materials, and more particularly if new equipment is needed, for example cameras or a CD-ROM drive. At the day-to-day level, priorities can be defined and a timetable of action, couched in terms of teaching and learning, can be made explicit.

Action plan: co-ordination

A well-constructed rationale for art can also lead to a proper deployment of resources and strengths within the school. These can then be seen to match the needs of art, particularly if shared teaching or shared equipment is required. In some schools issues related to staff development can also be seen to rely on well-structured development plans; for example the school's priorities in terms of Inset can best be prioritised by this process. In many schools there is a need for teachers to improve their knowledge and skills in teaching attainment target 2 of the National Curriculum for Art, and a good rationale can highlight this requirement and match it against other Inset needs of other teachers and other curriculum areas.

Action plan: communication

One of the great strengths of formulating a sound rationale is that the process involves wide consultation, discussion and feedback from colleagues, resulting in a greater sense of unity of purpose between teachers. An obvious benefit here is to consolidate the ethos which underpins the school and to break down barriers between those people who, for very good reasons of their own, do not always understand the aims and purposes of other people's teaching of art. It is of utmost importance for art co-ordinators and teachers to be articulate in their communications with parents, new teachers and governors, outside support staff and those agencies outside the school such as OFSTED inspectors and LEA officials, as well as the wider community. For example, it is not unusual to exhibit children's art work in public buildings. Artist in residence schemes are a good example of how, recently, artists of all kinds have communicated about their art by working with children in schools. Poets and musicians as well as visual artists often feature as part of the arts curriculum and also act as catalysts in supporting work for cross-curricular themes such as equal opportunities and multi-cultural understanding. Art can thereby be seen to communicate ideas and values that are not 'art for art's sake' but relate to larger issues within society and culture.

Action plan: evaluation

The process of continuous self-evaluation is also dependent on a properly constructed set of aims and objectives which reflect the principles and practice of the art programme. This is necessary not only for internal purposes of good reflective practice and the organic development of lively work, but also in respect of the external evaluation by OFSTED or the LEA. Naturally, the process of evaluation will lead to further planning and start the cycle once again.

In discussing a school's objectives for development our comments have been general and would apply to the majority of primary schools. However, the way in which primary schools deal with curriculum subjects in general, and art in particular, will vary.

ART: SUBJECT OR TOPIC FOCUS, OR BOTH?

Since the introduction of the National Curriculum most primary schools have had to reassess the way in which they deal with particular subjects. The methods which had become the orthodoxy since the Plowden Report of the 1960s have been brought into question by recent legislation. During the last twenty years a great variety of practices in primary schools, such as whole class teaching, group work, peer group teaching and the integrated day have all been tried and tested with various levels of success. The introduction of a subject centred curriculum has meant a re-evaluation of these practices. The position of art in the curriculum has changed and, probably for the first time in some schools, attention has to be paid to its nature as a discipline as well as a means through which a variety of learning can take place. The 1993 OFSTED report, *Curriculum Organisation and Classroom Practice in Primary Schools*, outlined the relationship between topic work and subject work. It did not deal with art as such, but it provides a useful snapshot to assess the current situation. The survey, based on observations in 70 primary schools in 1992, states:

> The vast majority of primary schools remain firmly committed to grouping aspects of different subjects together to be taught as 'topics'. All the schools except one taught some or much of the curriculum through topics or themes. Over the year, however, there was a noticeable shift towards designing topics that were more focused on a single subject, such as history or science; fewer schools than previously use broad topics to teach all or most of the subjects. Over half of the schools had a policy of planning topic work on a whole school basis involving one, two or three year cycles.
>
> (OFSTED 1993: 8)

Although the evidence for the above survey was gathered in 1992, it is our view that the drift towards subject centred teaching continued until the National Curriculum was revised by the Dearing Committee. Currently, it appears that the tendency is to re-evaluate topic work as a means of delivering part of the art curriculum, so the debate regarding subject focus or thematic focus is still alive. Most primary schools seem to adopt a mixture of both practices for pragmatic reasons.

How does art fare in this constantly shifting pattern? It may be a single subject taught by a specialist teacher in specialist premises and have very specific outcomes based on clear objectives. It may be part of a thematic project dealing with England in the 1930s, for instance, or part of an expressive arts programme related to dance or drama where its focus might lie in personal, social and moral education. It may occur as part of a design project or a publicity campaign to advertise a special event. All these different contexts will have embedded within them particular teaching methods and learning objectives. Some might have art teaching as part of their principle aim, whilst others may be using art as a vehicle for some other purpose. Trying to map these various aspects of the subject is difficult and the territory complex. One of our objectives in this Unit is to identify various starting points and developments which can legitimately accommodate these different purposes and ensure coherence, continuity and progression.

Before these starting points can be established some kind of audit needs to take place which will give a fairly clear idea of the resources available in terms of staffing, staff expertise, time available, materials, equipment and space.

The next teacher activity requires you to work with your colleagues to make an audit of the art teaching and provision in your school. Figure 5.1 represents a midway process in such an analysis and is based on a hypothetical primary school with ten staff. Mr Phillips is an art co-ordinator and the staff have just begun the analysis of their brainstorming on the white-board.

TEACHER ACTIVITY 5.2

Audit

Put aside a staff meeting for this activity. As a whole staff, brainstorm the following talking point – 'art teaching and provision in our school'. Ask the scribe to write up this central phrase and the immediate responses that come from all members of staff, thinking as widely as possible about recent practice and provision. Pay particular attention to whether the art was taught as topic-related work or as a discrete subject.

You will find that the discussion provides plenty of evidence of recent practice and some of the areas that need attention. Place a time limit on this brainstorming process. Once finished, two members of staff will be required to make a systematic analysis of the data which will be presented to the staff at a follow-up meeting.

Analysis

Base your analysis upon the following headings, previously introduced under the action plan: planning, co-ordination, communication, evaluation. It should be noted printmaking – all classes – fine   NC AT2 problem all round. . .?

textiles. . .? who knows about this? = Gap

clay – class 4/5 = kiln problem

No ceramics Year 1/2

painting in all years – some taught as topic but most as art lessons

Art teaching and provision in our school

equipment problem in Class 6   resources for Year 1, especially big brushes

Impressionism / Greeks / England in 1930s

Class 6, no sink still!! help needed Thematic work years 1/2 /3/4 Subject focus Yr 5-6

1 Planning Need to organise firing of clay – rota – train Ms Jones. Inset for ceramics for all staff, Health and Safety regs for ceramics? Years 1/2 to consider whole class teaching for art on appropriate occasions. Critical studies Years 5/6 link to NC History Additional resources needed for AT2 (postcards, CD-ROM?).

2 Co-ordination Mr Phillips to co-ordinate firing rota (tell caretaker). Organise Inset for regular sessions 4.00pm. Set up CD-ROM Inset demo from LEA / HE?

3 Communication Inform head / governors about need for more Health and Safety training. Invite governors and parent rep to CD-ROM demo. Year 6 exhibition of art work for primary / secondary liaison in July.

4 Evaluation Still gaps in ceramics teaching, more staff required to take it on. Mr Phillips to evaluate learning benefits for children and report back to staff.

5 Other Parent (potter) Mr Leach expressed interest in taking clay club, Mr Phillips to liaise.

Figure 5.1 Primary school audit – art teaching

that some of the comments made by the teachers will not fit neatly under one heading but be interrelated and therefore appear under two or more headings.

After conducting your audit and analysis you will have discovered something about which parts of the art curriculum are taught as a topic or theme and which parts are taught as discrete subject lessons. These are not necessarily alternatives. Subject centred lessons can be taught as part of topic work, and topics can provide the content for subject centred lessons.

The advice in this book is mainly subject centred, but the OFSTED report mentioned earlier identifies factors associated with successful topic work. These factors will not surprise experienced teachers as they exemplify good practice, but they are worth consideration:

1   An agreed system of planning which is consistent and carefully structured, thus helping to ensure continuity and progression.
2   A degree of co-operation in planning which provides an opportunity for teachers to share the workload and their expertise.
3   Careful account taken of National Curriculum requirements (the programmes of study as well as the attainment targets). Topics are usually chosen to fit National Curriculum attainment targets and programmes of study, rather than the other way around. Attainment targets or aspects of attainment targets that do not fit in readily are taught separately.
4   Topics have a single subject bias or emphasise particular subjects.
5   Whole school agreement about subject coverage and the balance between subjects and topics, the outcomes of which are monitored by members of the senior management team.
6   The planning refers to learning outcomes or objectives, activities and assessment.

(OFSTED 1993: 21)

Our view is that certain factors in the above list – agreed systems of planning and co-operation, National Curriculum requirements, agreement about subject coverage, and about learning outcomes and assessment – apply equally to subject based work. The essential difference in subject centred work is that art itself directly drives the learning, and outcomes are measurable in artistic terms.

In the next section a synopsis of items covered in this book so far will give additional information about planning successful art centred programmes.

PROGRAMME DEVELOPMENT: REVIEW OF ITEMS COVERED AND ROUTES FORWARD

In the same way that teachers in school are asked to take stock of their curriculum in art in order to plan the way forward, so too is it necessary to take stock briefly of those items covered so far in this book that will assist in the task of programme development.

Items covered

Subject knowledge and understanding (Units 1 and 2)

- Be aware that your increasing knowledge of the subject will allow you to plan a greater range of appropriate programmes of study.
- Be clear of the relationship between art, craft and design in your planning.
- Ensure that the aims made explicit in your school's art rationale are incorporated in your planning.

The National Curriculum requirements to cover AT1, investigating and making and AT2, knowledge and understanding (Unit 2)

- Endeavour to link both attainment targets together where possible in your planning.
- Remember that the work with the children can start with either attainment target.
- Be clear that attainment target 1 (AT1) should engender a spirit of enquiry towards the interrelationship of recording, media and resources, and materials.
- Be clear that attainment target 2 (AT2) relates to the historical and critical study of art and artists in different contexts.
- Note that the formal elements of art relate to both attainment targets.
- Be aware of how children's reflection on and understanding of their own work and that of artists will contribute to their development in the subject.

Methods of teaching, learning and organising (Unit 3)

- Remember that children's self-reflection on their work is an intrinsic part of the making process.
- Be aware that the reflective spiral is developed through a foundation on which learning is based; the further development of ideas, skills or techniques; and an extension of the work through reflective evaluation of what has already been learned.
- Note that the reflective spiral applies to a teacher's individual and co-operative planning as well as the child's making process.
- Note that the learning process may be led by a new idea, a new medium, or a new technique.

The development of children's art work and their ability to appreciate art (Unit 4)

- Bear in mind that children's development is highly individual and only roughly conforms to models of development such as Lowenfeld's and Parsons'.
- Remember that all children's work will be influenced by their particular social and cultural context.
- Remember that teacher intervention will have an effect on children's development and that you have a positive role to play in teaching the subject.

Routes forward

In Unit 2 we considered problems of selecting appropriate subject matter from the vast store of knowledge, skills and activities encapsulated by art. It was suggested that in order to explore the relationship between the tradition and the developing child, a link was needed. The idea of 'touchstones' was suggested as giving some clue to the essentials that link both art and life. These touchstones included the relationship between people, especially within the family; enduring links with nature manifested in landscape, town-scape and seascape; the interiors of houses and the objects that surround us; our relationship with the animal kingdom; and most important of all, perhaps, our perception of ourselves as we feel we are and as we would like to be, including the religious and spiritual dimensions of our existence.

For the purposes of planning a programme, it is suggested that these touchstones can be further grouped together to provide three distinct routes.

Route 1 Concerned with subject matter and teaching method designed to develop the 'personal' aspects of the child's learning. This might include ideas to do with the self; spirituality; the immediate family; and relationships with other people and the local and global community.

Route 2 Concerned with the environment. This includes most observational work of natural and made objects; the landscape, seascape, townscape; weather and climatic conditions; and links with science that will draw attention to the world revealed through the microscope and the world revealed through the telescope.

Route 3 Cultural aspects which embrace the past and the present through the links with art and artists, historical periods and current practices in art. Further, this practice establishes the link between the child and other aspects of society such as history, citizenship and particular aspects of British and world cultures.

The expanding world of the child, although dominated initially by the family and the local environment and then by the culture as a whole, is bound to be influenced by things which occur in either of these sectors. The interaction which occurs naturally in the life of the child can be enhanced and developed by the programme of learning devised by the school. In art, the attainment targets reflect this interactive process and consequently form natural relationships between art and the learner.

Before considering in more detail the routes outlined here it is useful to restate that programmes in art may be constructed so that they emphasise a topic centred or subject centred approach, but that these are not mutually exclusive – each can be part of the other if required.

Route 1 The personal aspects of the child's learning

You know a great deal about the children in your class. Each day they will tell you things about their lives, details of their family and people they meet, pets they have and food they like to eat. They will tell you about their neighbours and what its like on their journey to school; about the corner shop and the lollipop lady. They will tell you of important events, like birthdays, often celebrated by the class, and holidays and visits to grandparents. Teachers also have access to more intimate aspects of their lives, their likes and dislikes, whom they love, whom they trust and sometimes whom they do not. Sometimes, teachers are acutely aware of sadness at a family death and joy and sometimes uncertainty at a family birth. The child's sense of how they see themselves in the world and their sense of well-being or uncertainty forms part of a teacher's understanding of the child. Art has a particular part to play in enabling the child to communicate some of the feelings embodied in their experience to themselves and to other people. Plate 8 shows a child's exploration of the notion of the wider global family. This notion is eloquently expressed by Rob Barnes:

> To be involved in creative activity is to confront how we feel about things. Expressing a mood, emotion, or temperament through art becomes as valid as responding to another person, a moving sight, or a meaningful experience. Both responding and expressing through art puts us in touch with qualities which are part of what makes us human. As such they give special significance and meaning to what we see with our eyes and the inner eye of the mind. They touch on part of us that nothing else can.
>
> (Barnes 1987: 1)

This is a good definition of a very rich territory and there are myriad ways of exploring it with purpose, all leading to potentially successful outcomes whether your starting point is

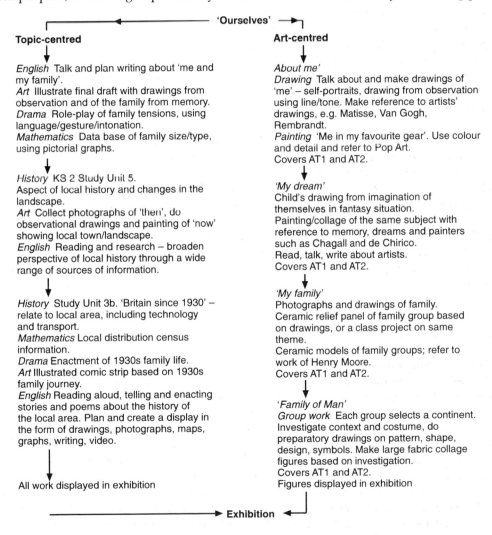

Figure 5.2 Route 1: Ourselves

topic or art centred. In Figure 5.2 we suggest one such example where both routes are developed. It indicates the two approaches that have been discussed. Both routes have the same starting point and conclusion. This example could be the result of brainstorming between members of staff and the art co-ordinator in order to devise one term's work for a year group, in this case Year 3. The following two terms would be planned to ensure continuity and progression.

Route 2   Children learn about their environment

Children display a natural curiosity about their immediate surroundings. They have intimate knowledge of their own homes, gardens, streets and shops and sometimes the route between home and school extends their understanding of a 'world' some distance from their home and yet joined to it. Their experience is strongly multi-sensory and immediate.

This domain of learning is logically encapsulated in the curriculum subjects of history, geography and science but is also firmly rooted in art. In their various ways, in different cultures and historical periods, artists have always drawn information and inspiration from their observable world. So too does the child. There seems to be some correspondence between the order and sequence of pattern, form and structure observable in nature and the way in which young children logically make marks and create images. This is developed more formally in school and, like mathematics and the development of language, has underpinning it a sense of order.

The development of seeing and understanding the environment leads to the growth of visual perception, in such a way that this world can often be codified according to the visual language of art. For example, organic structures, such as the leaves on a tree or pebbles on a beach, can be classified and then contrasted to geometric arrangements such as brick walls, tiled roofs, the shapes of windows and the joints in the pavement. The teacher has a particular role in pointing out the similarities in shape, pattern, form and structure.

This whole business of creating a sense of place and atmosphere in art is often based on the natural landscape and the built environment. In Britain in particular, the mood and atmosphere engendered by the weather not only influenced great painters such as Constable and Turner but can provide a powerful stimulus for children's drawing and painting.

Figure 5.3 might represent the result of brainstorming by staff and the art co-ordinator to provide one term's art programme for a year group, in this case Year 6. As suggested before, the work for the following two terms would need to ensure continuity and progression in all curriculum areas. It would also be possible to extend any of these examples over a much longer period of time.

Route 3   Children learn about the wider world, past and present

The child's access to the wider world is often via secondary sources such as television and film; from pictures, magazines and books; from conversations with adults; and from postcards of exotic places. Their knowledge of hospitals, churches, railway stations or airports may be formed by television programmes, long before they have any real

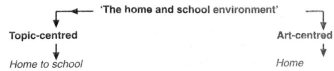

Topic-centred

Home to school

Art Talk about and draw routes to and from school, to different scales.
Maths 2D/3D scale models of classrooms showing school interior.
English History Study Unit 5 – research, read, write about the history of your school.

Outside the school – the building

History Study Unit 5 – further research. Collect old photographs from parents.
Art Draw exterior, shape, form, surface.
English Research, read, write about the past.
Geography Make plan or map to scale using symbols and keys. Use secondary sources, photographs (including aerial) and interview old girls and boys.
Science Classify materials and properties, investigate production of brick/concrete.

Outside the school – living things

Investigate school grounds.
Geography Make plans and maps in a variety of scales, collect secondary sources.
Art Draw and paint habitats within grounds, looking at small creatures/animals and their environment. Increase the scale. Develop into textiles using Batik techniques.
English Read about creatures/animals and draft, then write up your study of habitat/food chains.
Drama Role-play. Small production based on conflict and survival in creatures' ecosystem.
Mathematics/Information Technology Collect and represent data on creatures/animals.
Science Living things – adaptation. Investigate/research animals in different habitats. Investigate food chains in an ecosystem and relationship with green plants. Investigate operation of micro-organisms that positively assist creatures' survival.

Art-centred

Home

Drawing Draw the exterior of home, investigating shape, line, pattern, structure. Explore detail – bricks, tiles, windows. Refer to Vermeer, de Hooch, Canaletto drawings. Covers AT1 and AT2.

The house unfolded

Do a painting or collage of a section through a house or doll's house. Link to domestic activities. Construct a narrative. Refer to architectural drawings, paintings of Anthony Green. Covers AT1 and AT2.

Detail of built and natural environment

Examine through shape, form and texture. Use drawing, photography/video, rubbings. Examine details of windows, doors, drain covers, street furniture, etc. Develop into clay relief work, plaster casting, collagraphs. Refer to the Boyle Family's paintings and relief castings.

Explore the shape, form, texture, pattern of plants, leaves, pebbles, shells, etc. through monoprinting, clay, modelling, sculpture. Refer to medieval and Celtic art, and sculpture, (Hepworth, Nicholson). Covers AT1 and AT2.

Atmospheric painting (AT1 and AT2)

Paint a landscape or townscape. Create 'mood' paintings of thunderstorm, fire, blizzard through dramatic paint quality, technique, colour and tone. Refer to Constable, Lowry, Weight.

Large mural of the wider community

Our school and town, individual, group, class work. Painting/collage developed from observational work of buildings, streets, people, etc.

Exhibition in local secondary school

Figure 5.3 Route 2: The home and school environment

experience of them. The adult world of work will be known through parents, family and friends, each with their own perspective.

At what sometimes appears to be a frightening pace, our experiences and opinions about the world are often substantially formed before we encounter situations face-to-face, especially in this age of electronic, multimedia communication. To adapt a well-known phrase, never has so much been communicated to so many by so few! Potentially this offers a great opportunity for investigation and acquiring knowledge about the world. However, it also enables clichés and stereotypes about the world to be negatively reinforced.

One of the functions of education is to link children to the wider world in a spirit of enquiry so that they may be discriminating about their acquisition of knowledge and understanding. Traditionally, the link has been made largely through books, but technology is being harnessed to this task. One benefit of video and CD-ROM is that the technology has the potential to provide easy access to an exciting store of the world's art. This makes available an infinitely greater source than previously, providing information and provoking a sense of wonder and enquiry. What might be suitable touchstones in art to link children to the wider world of the present and the past? Encountering paintings, sculptures and craft work first-hand in exhibitions and galleries is important. So, too, is looking at reproductions of works of art, on paper and through video and CD-ROM, especially where access to first-hand sources is limited.

Because works of art often act as metaphors for particular cultures and display aspects of human behaviour, they can in themselves provide a touchstone for children. Through the analysis of pictures, objects and artefacts the child, supported by the teacher, can find factual, emotional and technical links with their own experiences and work. The analysis of a picture provides a method of unpacking a source of information, analysing its content, form, structure and the maker's view which underpins it. The painting will also, through its use of symbols and allegory, reflect a view of the world current at the time of its creation.

Using some of the analytical methods suggested in this book should help you to avoid the visual clichés and stereotypes that are often encountered when pupils are asked to investigate the wider world. This is particularly true when the events under discussion are charged with values that may or may not correspond to those held in the child's world. The relationship between children's home culture, that of the school and that of society is dynamic and interactive. One of the difficulties of educating children about their social and cultural heritage is somehow to relate their familiarity with their own sense of place to the diversity and complexity of the many different cultures that together make up Britain's collective culture. In modern Britain there may be a 'dominant' culture, but room and respect must be given to those groups within society which have a network of beliefs, customs, habits and behaviours vital to their identity.

Teachers have the task of selecting from a huge menu those items which are appropriate to the needs of the pupils in their classes. Even within the confines of the National Curriculum there is the opportunity for children to come to terms with and learn about a cultural heritage which is rich and diverse.

Art can play an important part in helping pupils to understand cultural diversity by bringing them into contact with the behaviours, attitudes and values of their own and others' cultures. The recognition of shared, common media, processes and techniques across the globe and through time, can link disparate cultures. Further, remembering that works

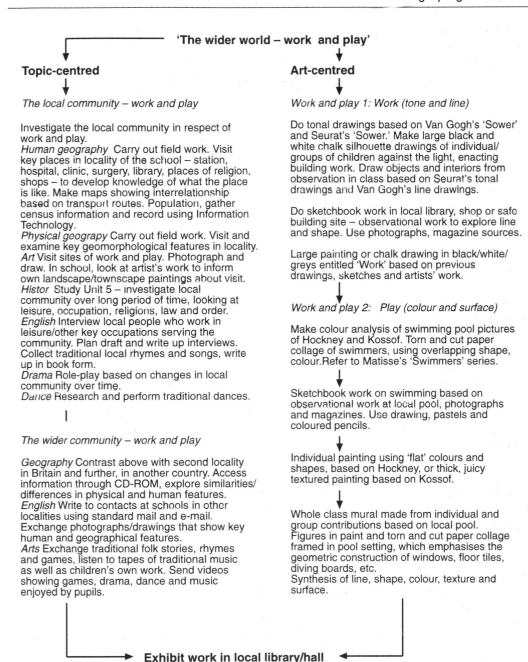

'The wider world – work and play'

Topic-centred

The local community – work and play

Investigate the local community in respect of work and play.
Human geography Carry out field work. Visit key places in locality of the school – station, hospital, clinic, surgery, library, places of religion, shops – to develop knowledge of what the place is like. Make maps showing interrelationship based on transport routes. Population, gather census information and record using Information Technology.
Physical geograpy Carry out field work. Visit and examine key geomorphological features in locality.
Art Visit sites of work and play. Photograph and draw. In school, look at artist's work to inform own landscape/townscape paintings about visit.
Histor Study Unit 5 – investigate local community over long period of time, looking at leisure, occupation, religions, law and order.
English Interview local people who work in leisure/other key occupations serving the community. Plan draft and write up interviews. Collect traditional local rhymes and songs, write up in book form.
Drama Role-play based on changes in local community over time.
Dance Research and perform traditional dances.

The wider community – work and play

Geography Contrast above with second locality in Britain and further, in another country. Access information through CD-ROM, explore similarities/ differences in physical and human features.
English Write to contacts at schools in other localities using standard mail and e-mail. Exchange photographs/drawings that show key human and geographical features.
Arts Exchange traditional folk stories, rhymes and games, listen to tapes of traditional music as well as children's own work. Send videos showing games, drama, dance and music enjoyed by pupils.

Art-centred

Work and play 1: Work (tone and line)

Do tonal drawings based on Van Gogh's 'Sower' and Seurat's 'Sower.' Make large black and white chalk silhouette drawings of individual/ groups of children against the light, enacting building work. Draw objects and interiors from observation in class based on Seurat's tonal drawings and Van Gogh's line drawings.

Do sketchbook work in local library, shop or safe building site – observational work to explore line and shape. Use photographs, magazine sources.

Large painting or chalk drawing in black/white/ greys entitled 'Work' based on previous drawings, sketches and artists' work.

Work and play 2: Play (colour and surface)

Make colour analysis of swimming pool pictures of Hockney and Kossof. Torn and cut paper collage of swimmers, using overlapping shape, colour. Refer to Matisse's 'Swimmers' series.

Sketchbook work on swimming based on observational work at local pool, photographs and magazines. Use drawing, pastels and coloured pencils.

Individual painting using 'flat' colours and shapes, based on Hockney, or thick, juicy textured painting based on Kossof.

Whole class mural made from individual and group contributions based on local pool. Figures in paint and torn and cut paper collage framed in pool setting, which emphasises the geometric construction of windows, floor tiles, diving boards, etc.
Synthesis of line, shape, colour, texture and surface.

Exhibit work in local library/hall

Figure 5.4 Route 3: The wider world – work and play

of art often represent in symbolic form the values of a particular culture or sub-culture, there is a natural relationship between art and history and the more personal social, moral and spiritual education of children through the interrogation of works of art. A historical and critical studies programme is essential in order to link the work of artists to the child's own work and to provide insights into the conditions which generated the original painting, sculpture or artefact.

In looking at a painting the child has the opportunity to open a window on to the world. For instance, Picasso's *Guernica* (Figure 2.3) illustrates horses, bulls and weeping people, but more profoundly, through its use of metaphor, its technique and its composition, it describes the horror of wanton destruction, of human life thrown away.

Art can also be used to explore the changes that take place in society over time. A class visit to a mainline railway station will bring alive its history and purpose. The building's design will provide insights into the developments in engineering which were needed to meet the requirements of a mobile and affluent society of the nineteenth century. A study of Frith's painting, *Paddington Station*, can be used to contrast the past to the present day. Observation of the staff and passengers, both in this painting and in life, will give rise to insights into the diverse nature of our society as well as the changing technologies.

In devising Figure 5.4 we are aware that it represents only a minute proportion of what might be covered. There is an infinite number of ways in which first-hand experience can be combined with artistic analysis. Again, this example focuses on one term's work, or longer, and would be followed by further activities that logically ensure continuity and progression. On the other hand, parts of the example could be expanded into much longer units. This example is aimed at Year 4 and Year 5 pupils. All the art-centred work integrates the two attainment targets AT1 and AT2.

These three routes may give some guidance to art co-ordinators who have to begin planning programmes for art for the various year groups. As experienced teachers you will find the cross-curricular planning, based on National Curriculum requirements, fairly straightforward. What may be more challenging is relating the requirements for art to your topic in a way that ensures continuity and progression and can lead to planning a route entirely for art. The following teacher activity is designed to give an art co-ordinator an opportunity to devise a programme for art in the context of his or her own school with its particular needs.

   TEACHER ACTIVITY 5.3

In preparation for this activity re-read the National Curriculum document for art. Pay close attention to the programmes of study as well as the attainment targets. Examine the 'end of key stage' descriptions which are designed to help you judge your pupil's attainment against your learning objectives.

Second, re-read the factors associated with successful topic work, remembering that many of these apply to planning for art.

Third, re-read the analysis made from activity 5.2 in order to remind yourself of the nature of your school's and staff's needs in relation to teaching art. At this stage, do not worry about differentiation or assessment as these matters will be covered in some depth in the next unit. Draft a rough plan, the final detail of which will be developed later.

1   Assuming that your school bases its planning on topic work, acquire the programme for the next term, which may already make reference to art activities designed to support learning in art and other curriculum areas.
2   Draft a programme for art that has a starting point within the topic but that looks entirely at learning objectives in art and that:

-    contains a balance of first-hand experience and work from secondary sources
-    ensures integration of the two attainment targets
-    ensures that pupils have the opportunity to look at artists' work
-    ensures a balance of 2-D and 3-D work
-    ensures that pupils have the opportunity to work in different scales
-    allows pupils to work individually, in groups and as a whole class
-    concentrates on the core art activities of drawing and painting, and some craft work (for example, one area of textiles, printmaking or 3-D)

After finishing your draft ask a colleague to read it and to see if it makes sense in terms of the above points. If you think you are on the right lines, draft work for the following two terms and then check to see if the programme allows for continuity and encourages progression.

SUMMARY

In this Unit we have assumed that every school has its own ethos and organisational structure which is dependent on local circumstances and a relationship to the community it serves. It is also assumed that these are desirable and that the richness and diversity of primary education can still be maintained within the National Curriculum requirements. Objectives for planning and development are discussed in the context of producing a well-constructed rationale for art which clearly sets out the school's policy, practices and values. Practical advice is outlined on how to develop action plans stemming from the rationale to facilitate teaching and learning. A structure for planning, co-ordination, communication and evaluation has been offered, with the aim of bringing this action plan into being. Suggestions are made regarding curriculum audit and how to establish planning routes which accommodate a sound rationale, a choice of topic- or art-centred approaches and material resources. These routes have been developed in some detail, with practical examples based on three foci – the personal aspects of children's learning, their relationship to their immediate environment and their relationship to the broader culture. Within these routes particular attention has been paid to the National Curriculum. In the following Unit, this planning will be built on and linked to differentiation and assessment in art.

Planning classroom activities with assessment in mind

In Unit 5, outlines and activities were suggested for planning a programme in art through a variety of routes with a different emphasis in each. Underpinning these suggestions was the relationship between the development of the formal elements of art and the study of its critical and contextual aspects. In this Unit, these ideas are explored further through sample schemes and lessons which are intended to offer insights into ways that particular ideas can be expanded.

VISUAL LITERACY AND CRITICAL STUDIES

To be visually literate implies a capacity to appreciate and discriminate what is seen by the eye. This ability is learned. In the same way that literacy implies a capacity to appreciate and manipulate language, so too visual literacy implies the ability to 'read' visual images. This type of 'reading' includes the ability to draw meaning from symbols, signs, diagrams, road signs, maps, posters, computer icons and works of art. Visual literacy also implies the maker's capacity to communicate through the use of images. It implies a capacity to be critically appreciative of all objects and artefacts that have been designed and made, such as cars, clothing, household goods. At a deeper level it implies the ability to understand such cultural symbols as works of art. Visual literacy can be seen as a universal need but, like literacy, it is culturally determined and education must acknowledge and accommodate this fact.

An ability to be critically appreciative allows us to make informed and discriminating choices about the things that surround us, that we buy or go to see. Visual literacy is acquired through experience and education. The combination of seeing and doing during the educative process includes close observation of our surroundings and practical activities designed to increase our perception of what is seen.

In Picasso's work, for example, we can observe an immense capacity to manipulate what he saw into endless new artistic configurations. Visual literacy of a very high order is at work here. As a result not only of immense ability but also intensive education in art and the history of art at a very early age, he developed a capacity to appear like an 'old master' at the age of 14. For Picasso, 'seeing' and 'doing' formed a reciprocal cycle which in turn developed and reinforced his capacity to be visually literate.

Seeing images is an everyday event, but looking in a more analytical way can yield aesthetically satisfactory experiences which denote a relationship between natural objects, manufactured goods, and works of art. There is a observable relationship between the rounded forms of pebbles, a well-designed wash basin and a Barbara Hepworth sculpture.

Active and purposeful observation of the world, together with artistic activities, develop an appreciation of the formal elements of art such as line, tone and colour. This appreciation in turn reinforces the perceptual cycle.

Additionally, the relationship between art, craft and design needs to be addressed in the context of visual perception. Although we may view a painting, a chair and a computer with the same critical eye, their respective functions also have a part to play in the way we view them. For example, the symbolic and expressive aspects of a painting reciprocate with the way we view it and form part of the perceptual activity. Similarly, the function, material and visual qualities of the chair or computer focus and extend our perception of these also. What they all share is the capacity to be perceived as aesthetically satisfactory objects.

These kind of perceptions and the development of visual literacy are helpful in appreciating the world in which we live because they form the basis of aesthetic experience. In the context of this book, what is required is to have artistic experience and develop artistic appreciation. A view of a mountain or a stream may well provide great pleasure, but to view a *painting* of the mountain or the stream we need a means whereby the forms and symbols of art, which underpin the subject matter, can also be read. In teaching, this capacity is developed through the children's process of making drawings and paintings, presenting the paintings to the children and an audience, talking about them and evaluating what has been done before the work is developed further.

Visual literacy can also be developed by studying others' art works. The strategies for analysing works of art logically, in full and in depth, have already been alluded to in this book, and are based on the work of Rod Taylor (1986, 1993).

No discussion of critical studies, however brief, would be complete without a repetition of Taylor's system for analysing pictures in the educational context. His approach to the study of form, content, process, mood, encompasses in a straightforward manner the procedures that have always formed the substance of learning about art through art. The model works well with works of art which have some narrative, symbolic or expressive characteristics, such as painting or sculpture; interestingly, the model can also be applied to other art forms, such as drama and music. Taylor wrote:

Four fundamental areas all have teaching potential and should beneficially form the basis of any accompanying support information. They are relevant to all art and craft objects, though the emphasis on particular aspects will inevitably vary from work to work.

The areas are:

1   Content: The work's content in terms of subject matter, how significant this is and how the artist had accumulated the necessary information, etc.
2   Form: The formal qualities of the work in terms of its arrangement into shapes, structure and colour organisation, etc.
3   Process: The techniques, processes and methods – and time-scales – involved in the making of the work.
4   Mood: The mood, atmosphere and feelings evoked by the work.

(Taylor 1993: 25)

The straightforward approach and all-embracing nature of this model for analysing works of art make it ideal for teaching and learning.

The work of Rod Taylor referred to above was carried out when he directed the Critical Studies in Art Education Project at the notable Drumcroon Education Art Centre in Wigan. This centre was designed to serve the community; it welcomed primary and secondary pupils from schools and was open to the general public. The centre's policy statement and its aims were as follows:

To give all Wigan's young people – irrespective of age – their teachers and the local community access to the range, breadth and variety of the visual arts through the focus of contemporary makers, taking into account such issues as those of race, gender and special needs. To give further insight and understanding the centre provides its visitors with opportunities to engage in related practical activities and it also attempts to place each exhibition into a contextual framework by demonstrating processes through resident artists and craftspeople and through the use of secondary source material which has the potential to range across time, place and cultures.

Embedded within this policy statement is a framework for excellent aims and practice as far as art teaching and learning is concerned. By concentrating examples on the work of contemporary makers it provided children with a culture which sees art as a living language with something to say about their life and times, and in addition it gave them insight into the traditions which underpin the contemporary artist's work. The statement about race, gender and special needs can be viewed as a commitment to people's rights in art education and, by its very nature, takes a non-elitist view toward art and access to it. An important issue is how the process of art making is linked to an understanding of the subject through the work of artists and craftspeople, and how this makes positive links to a wider cultural context. Importantly it talks of the use of secondary source material like reproductions, postcards, videos and slides, which can range across time, place and cultures, opening up a world-wide perspective on what might be 'suitable' subject matter for teaching and learning in art.

The project also threw up two key issues which have been part of the fabric of this book. These issues flow from the necessity of students to become involved with viewing works of art, visiting exhibitions and galleries, and looking at reproductions of paintings and other related sources.

First is the issue of what Taylor (1986) calls the 'illuminating experience' – when an individual is so overwhelmed by a work of art that it gives them a startling new insight and a sense of revelation. Attention is concentrated and there is a retained memory of the event. There is an 'arousal of appetite' for gaining greater insight into the work and thc conditions that influenced its making. Additionally, a heightened sense of environmental awareness is gained, which in educational terms can link the study of art to the practice of making art.

The second issue is that of contextualization. This is concerned with the relationship between an artist's work, and other work which may be associated with it. For example, an understanding of Constable's 1821 painting *The haywain* may be enhanced by a visit to an exhibition of nineteenth century agricultural implements and costumes, studying some examples of the poetry of Wordsworth and other English Romantic poets, learning about cloud formations, reading stories about the working horse and looking at photographs of the East Anglian countryside. This is an example of a contextualization within art and, to a certain extent, across the arts. This method, related to any work of art, can be repeated and extended to include newspaper cuttings of contemporary events, music and appropriate historical documents. In teaching terms, contextualization is often the stuff of display.

Children's work can be similarly developed in order to support and extend their ideas and learning. Skilful use of contextual studies and display can provide children with clues so that they may see their work in relation to other associated material. Sometimes contextual work can be regarded as a detective story or a crossword puzzle leading to the child's broader understanding of their own work. For instance, the 'Children's games' programme in Unit 2 (page 32) would provide a good contextual framework for children's learning because it incorporates a reproduction of a work of art, children's photographic and sketch book work, role-play through drama, investigating and collecting information from magazines and postcards and making reference to several artists. This project firmly links the past to the present and encompasses science and writing, which helps to broaden the context of the children's learning and adds breadth and depth to their understanding of art and other subjects.

Visual literacy and critical studies operate together, each enhancing the other. This way of learning shares an authenticity with the way many artists make their work. In the case of both artist and child, a learning process of generating an idea, developing, synthesising and refining it takes place, resulting in an artefact of some sort being produced. Below, artist Alan Richards discusses the development of a series of paintings based on war. His explanation of the work shows how, in his painting, both visual literacy and perception, and critical and contextual references, play an intrinsic part in the creative process:

 You know that lovely hill behind the Bowd Inn on the way to Sidmouth? What I wanted to do was a set of paintings based on the dreadful state of affairs in what was Yugoslavia, they are about war. It came to me when I was watching television that there was this beautiful landscape in full colour, rather Cézanne-like, with little red roofs. It was like a rather beautiful pen and colour drawing and then suddenly, one of the roofs was blown off and you realised you weren't looking at Provence, you were looking at Bosnia. It just occurred to me that if I was to find some landscapes which were beautiful and shift the emphasis I could say something about war, but not obviously, like some of the paintings you can see in the Imperial War Museum where people are blown up.

The titles of the three pictures I painted are *The onset of winter − sowing and planting, The onset of winter 2 − after the reaping* and third, *Now is the winter of our discontent.* Isn't it curious that when we talk about war we talk in agricultural terms.

We talk about men being 'mown down'. It's the reverse of terms that are normally concerned with growth and life. The first painting [Plate 9] is about the planting of mines. To plant a mine is an obscenity. I've taken from Millet the figure of the sower and the two figures who are, in my painting, planting mines. The sower is obviously Death and he is casting a shadow across these two men who are vaguely in battle dress, doing the planting. But the landscape is simply taken from the back road to Sidmouth.

The second painting [Plate 10] has an awful kind of angularity about it, the reaping of a whole generation on the battlefields ... the fires in this painting are not the fires of burning off the stubble of a well-husbanded landscape, they are the 'fire of battle' that is moving through the landscape and they are about ethnic cleansing.

What we see at work here is a powerful imagination that enables Alan to link his own work to first-hand experience of the landscape filtered through his knowledge of both art and contemporary events. There is a quality of thinking and creativity present which has been developed through visual literacy and knowledge of art, synthesised and applied in a particular context of painting. It is this quality of knowledge, skill and understanding which we should aim to engender in children's learning. The means of achieving this, according to Taylor, are through working with artists, gallery visits, working from reproductions and learning from art in a variety of different contexts. Visual literacy, and aesthetic and artistic understanding, should develop from this approach.

ASSESSMENT IN ART

If by the end of this Unit you have developed a scheme of practical activities that ensure development of children's visual literacy through critical studies you will need to decide how you will assess that development.

Can art be assessed?

In our view, most decidedly, yes. The confusion in people's minds has grown from the belief that if art is about feeling, then the individual experience of making, viewing, and understanding it is personal, subjective and therefore beyond the realm of objective assessment by others. This debate has been well aired in the last decade, and rightly so. Including a subject in the National Curriculum that involves work so subjective that it cannot be assessed by teachers would be a nonsense, and would leave art as an unimportant 'frill' rather than a body of knowledge.

David Best suggests, 'My central concern can be stated simply: if artistic judgments cannot be rationally, objectively justified there can be no place for the arts in education' (Best 1992: xvi). This unequivocal statement is consistent with comments he made seven years before, when he stated:

 That artistic understanding is rooted in natural response does *not* imply that there are no criteria for the appropriateness of responses to particular works of art; that is to say, it does not imply that there are no limits to the kinds of feeling or attitude which an individual may appropriately have.

(Best 1985: 8)

Best suggests that artistic feelings are expressions of certain kinds of understanding which help us interpret what we are looking at, whether it is a pot we are making or a painting made by an artist. We are using reason to make our interpretations and Best suggests, therefore, that artistic feelings are rational in kind. In making a 'natural response' we are involved in making judgements which may be personal but are still judgements. These artistic judgements must be capable of being rationally justified to others if they are to maintain an accountable position in education.

In Unit 1 we introduced you to ways of reading a picture which gave certain objective starting points on which to base an interpretation of paintings. Your role as teacher is to enable children to interpret works of art, using similar strategies. By working with children in this way you will be able to find out if they are able to make artistic judgements themselves in relation to their own work and the work of others.

Who is the assessment for?

Assessment in art education, as in any other subject, serves to inform the teacher, the child and the parents about the child's progress. Formative assessment is of particular importance in art as it serves the function of making the learning that is taking place explicit to the child. It will uncover attitudes and behaviours that may need developing, encouraging and extending. Furthermore, teacher and child will establish a language for talking about art, using the formal elements of art, that will in turn support the child's development in art. Summative assessment will probably take place when a particular individual, group or class project reaches a conclusion. It may be conducted with an individual child, a small group or the whole class.

How can art be assessed?

A framework for art assessment should guide the teacher in the formative as well as the summative assessment of the children's work. Also, the framework must be flexible enough to take into account art, craft and design and the diverse nature of art activity, a point made by Bob Clement:

The nature and range of the tasks we set children within art and design do require us to adopt a more flexible system of assessment than other subjects may require – it must be obvious that you cannot assess by the same criteria tasks as various as making a colour chart, modelling a figure in clay, illustrating a poem or painting a dream.

(Clement 1986: 233)

A further consideration is the need to take into account the child's immediate environment and cultural background. Veronica Treacher, in her summary and overview of research conducted into assessment in the arts, commented:

The teachers expressed their conviction that fair assessment had to take account of the many and varied experiences that children brought with them into the classroom, and to continually adapt and extend criteria for judgments in the light of new understandings. The accounts refer to the need to be aware of and responsive to the pupils' varied personal, social and cultural backgrounds – the antecedents of art.

(Treacher 1989: 218)

Before the National Curriculum was established, Rob Barnes contributed some useful guidelines for the assessment of art in the primary school. He suggests five categories that should be addressed when assessing children's art work. Each of the categories has a variety of criteria for forming judgements:

1 Process of working

This covers the important aspects of artistic development during the action of creating art work. Certain abilities like developing an idea, changing the design, substituting, adding and improving are not otherwise evident except during the process of working. Response to ideas and visual stimuli are sometimes far more evident during the process than they are in the final product.

2 Handling of materials

It is important to know whether or not children have developed good organisational skills and can use a variety of materials appropriately. This is quite without regard to the artistic outcomes. We need, for instance, to know if children can organise and use paints as a prerequisite to producing a worthwhile painting, or scissors if they are cutting out a shape. Otherwise there is a considerable gap between intention and skill needed to handle materials.

3 Use of media

Apart from the control of materials we need to know whether or not children are developing an understanding of the media they use. Can they, for example, mix colours together to produce shades? Do they simply draw with paint or can they use it in other ways (e.g. to produce textures, patterns, blocks of colour)? Can they design models in clay which make the best use of the medium?

(Barnes 1987: 164)

It can be seen that Barnes' first three categories fit into attainment target 1 of National Curriculum for Art, and the following fourth category sits nicely in attainment target 2:

4 Critical skills

This category deals with discriminatory skills and is concerned with looking and analysing. Children not only produce artwork, they develop the ability to discriminate between one colour and another, different lines and different shapes. They can be involved from an early age with looking at designs and artwork by other artists as well as their own work. They will also need to look at their natural environment in a critical way, comparing such varied designs and patterns as those on leaves or sea shells. Critical skills can also include self-assessment for which older children (7 to 9 years) might use a self-assessment sheet.

(Barnes 1987: 164)

His final category takes into account the need for teachers to know about and understand children's stages of personal development:

5 Stages of personal development
This covers assessment in relation to the expected stages for the age-range. As Eisner (1972) says, these stages are simply an indication of what children might be expected to do when left to their own devices. In order to make judgments we need to refer to stages of developing imagery but bear in mind that the aim is not to rush children through these stages. The aim is to see how far they have developed as a result of engaging in artwork. Besides this, there are social and personal attitudes to art such as the degree to which children value their own and other children's work. To what extent, for example, are they able to accept praise and criticism of their own work?

(Barnes 1987: 164)

We feel that Barnes' categories offer teachers a sound basis for assessment, in that they sensitively take into account the process of art making as well as the final product and they try to address the wide nature of the subject.

The National Curriculum has also addressed these issues through 'end of key stage' descriptions which set out the standard of performance expected of the majority of pupils at the end of each key stage. These descriptions form the basis for a general picture of a child's development and can be phrased as questions for the class teacher to address, as in the following example based on the end of key stage descriptions for key stage 2.

Key stage 2: questions to aid assessment of children's art work

Attainment target 1 – can the child:

1   record what they have experienced and imagined, expressing ideas and feelings confidently?
2   represent chosen features of the world around them with increasing accuracy and attention to detail?
3   select relevant resources and materials, and experiment with ideas that are suggested by these?
4   choose materials, methods and visual elements appropriate to their intentions, making images and artefacts for different purposes?
5   reflect on and adapt their work, identifying ways it can be developed and improved?

Attainment target 2 – can the child:

6   compare images and artefacts, using art, craft and design vocabulary, and identify similarities and differences in methods and approaches?
7   begin to recognise how works of art, craft and design are affected by their purpose, including, where appropriate, the intentions of the artist, crafts person or designer, and the time and place in which they are made?
8   evaluate their own and others' work in the light of what was intended?

The following teacher activity asks you to examine the National Curriculum for Art and identify how the end of key stage descriptions build in progression and ensure continuity.

TEACHER ACTIVITY 6.1

With a colleague, read the end of key stage descriptions for key stage 1. Divide up the various strands as in the example above, but as statements rather than questions. Then relate the strands to the end of key stage descriptions for key stage 2 to see how they make explicit a gradual development. This exercise will yield valuable information and give you some clear criteria for assessment. Type up the strands for dissemination amongst the staff and timetable a staff meeting for discussion.

The relationship between assessment and the process of children's art making

In Unit 3 we introduced the idea of children following an observable process when engaging in art activities (page 38). In Figure 6.1 we return to the process and suggest how assessment can be used to support children's learning at various stages in the process. Certain key questions for teachers are suggested in order to support children's learning.

Key questions A

1   'How is your idea coming along?'
     This question is based on the criteria in Barnes' category 1, 'process of working'. Children should be encouraged to talk about how the idea is developing, whether they

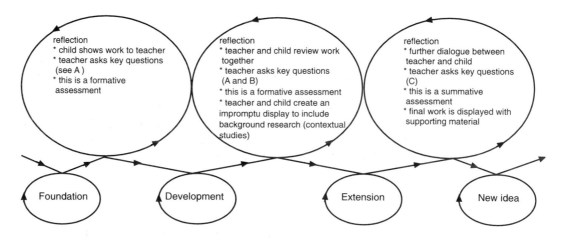

Figure 6.1 The reflective spiral – with key assessment questions

may feel a need to change the design, substitute another, identify other ways of improving the work, and so on. A close examination of the child's investigative work and research can be made around an impromptu display, laid out on a table or quickly pinned to the wall. This creates a good opportunity for shared discussion among peers, as well as between teacher and child, and demonstrates clearly the working process in terms of looking, thinking and doing.

2   'Do you want to practise more, or find out more about this material?'
This question may allow children who are struggling with using a particular medium to benefit from opportunities to experiment further with materials and equipment. This will build their confidence, increase their skill level and narrow the gap between intention and performance, as suggested by Barnes' second category, 'handling of materials'.

3   'Do you think you know more about using this (medium) now?'
Children should be encouraged to make explicit what they have learned about the medium, as suggested by Barnes' third category. In addition, this question will build skills of self-evaluation and the teacher should be prepared to extend the child's initial response. For example, the child may well answer, 'Yes, I like clay now', in which case the teacher needs to probe a little further − 'Tell me exactly why you like using clay now? What will it let you do ?'

4   'What is going to happen next?'
This question will require the child to organise and formulate the next stage of the work and also allow the teacher to see how he or she can best support development. Obviously, some children may need considerable guidance from their teacher but they should be encouraged to take as much of the responsibility for the decisions as possible. The child who painted the picture inspired by Picasso (Plate 11) made the painting after studying the artist's work, looking at shape, colour and composition.

Key question B

1   'Have you thought about artists who work in this way?'
This question will give the child an opportunity to make connections between their work and the work of other artists. They might find connections about the idea behind the work (that is, the maker's intention), or the subject matter, the medium or technique being used, the mood of the work or the formal qualities in the work. Obviously this will need some preparatory work on the part of the teacher, who will of course have just the right artist's work to hand! After discussion the child may want to extend the work in some way, having been influenced by the artist's work.

Key questions C

1   'Do you think the work is finished now, or is there more you think you can do?'
This question, framed within the context of positive suggestions from the teacher, will

give the child the opportunity to decide whether the work has reached a satisfactory conclusion or not. If not, the child may need further advice and support from the teacher.

2   'What do you really like about your finished piece?'
This will give the child the chance to sum up feelings of satisfaction about the work and build the critical skills mentioned in both Barnes' and Taylor's work. It is important to remember that these skills take time to develop in children, and the child will need a good model in a teacher who has thought carefully about how to appraise and talk about art.

3   'What have you learned about (colour, shape, line, form, pattern, texture, tone) in doing this work?'
This will draw the child's attention to their growing ability to handle the elements of art and also help them in utilising this special vocabulary of art to describe their own and other's work.

4   'Have you achieved what you hoped to achieve?'
This will require the child to consider their original intention and to see if the process has come to a satisfying conclusion. Children can be very self-critical and it often depends on the teacher helping the child to recognise certain developed strengths.

5   'Can you suggest a way of displaying the work to its best advantage?'
Behind this question is the notion that children should be directly involved in the process of making a display, from composing the structure and deciding on colour and style, to writing any explanatory text. It should be made explicit to children that the display will communicate to others about the work, showing not only the final piece but aspects of the investigative and research work (the contextual studies). A piece of work is seen to advantage when well-mounted and displayed, and children will come to realise that exhibition allows the maker a new distance from the work so that it can be more dispassionately and critically appraised. In this sense, display forms an integral part of the making process.

6   'Have you got any ideas about what you might do next, to develop the idea in a different way?'
This will give the child a chance to reflect on the learning so far and consider possible ways of developing it further, maybe on a different track.

These questions offer a basis for teacher and child discussion, through which assessment can be made both by the child and the teacher. Obviously the questions do not have to proceed in the order above. For example, many children actually start work by looking at the work of an artist, which might then lead to practical work, so the initial questions would be based on the approach suggested in Teacher Activity 1.1 (page 12) or 2.1 (page 26), or on Taylor's system for analysing pictures – content, form, process, mood (page 86).

At the stage of summative assessment it would be prudent to look again at the National Curriculum end of key stage descriptions before making a more formal assessment of the child's progress. In addition, you will need to reflect on whether your aims and learning objectives have been achieved, or how they could be improved. It will also help you to plan the work ahead in a way that will maximise benefit to children's learning.

DIFFERENTIATION

The National Curriculum for Art (1995) states that the revised document provides teachers with a greater flexibility to 'respond to the needs of pupils with identified special educational needs' and further, 'increases the scope for teachers to provide such pupils with appropriately challenging work at each key stage' (DFE 1995: v). In addition to this, there is a section to describe pupils whose attainment designates them as showing 'exceptional performance'. These pupils will also need specific programmes to challenge them and ensure that they, too, continue to develop their understanding, knowledge and skills. Interestingly, in our experience, the key to helping children often lies in giving them further opportunity to experiment. This could be within media or processes they already know; but asking them to experiment with a different scale or use the media in a different way will challenge them to think about a different aspect of the work without changing its basic character.

Most importantly, talking to children about the work and helping them to identify critically strengths and weaknesses will build a self-reflecting ethos as well as a vocabulary to help them evaluate their own work. The artist Alan Richards, when talking about judging the success of his own painting, said:

> It's a matter of actually having an informed approach to the many levels of possibility that make a painting work. It can be the idea, it can be the scale, it can be the colour, it can be the actual handling of the material, all sorts of things. As far as students or children are concerned, I think that they can answer it by being very hard on themselves because it's actually the development of their own understanding which will, in the end, give them the potential to actually determine whether something is right or something is wrong, something works or doesn't work.

The strategies suggested in Unit 3 on how to help children talk about their work, especially children who are stuck, were formulated to enable children to take responsibility for their own decisions. The transcript below is of a student teacher who is also working towards the idea of supporting individual children in their art work. He recounts his teaching in school and talks about the need to make the children critical of their own work.

> I think that it is really important for them to be critical because as a child I wasn't taught to be and so I make sure the children I teach are. I found myself going around while they were working in their groups and saying, 'Well, what about this? Why don't you agree with her then?' and then to her, 'Why don't you agree with him?' and then actually got a discussion going until they had sorted it out. That made them evaluate and justify their actions.

Later in this Unit we suggest some support and extension exercises that may help further in supporting the class or individual children who need help in art making or appreciation of art.

The next section of this Unit suggests how to devise a scheme of work for art that puts in place a number of lessons. The scheme is designed to be taught either over a term or half a term and incorporates display and assessment.

DEVISING A SCHEME OF WORK

The purpose of the scheme is to establish clear aims and learning outcomes so that the art experience for the children in your class has variety yet depth, has continuity and ensures progression. It will help you work out what you are going to do, what the children will be doing, what resources you will need to prepare, what sort of displays you can anticipate and what form the formative and summative assessment might take.

In working out what you are going to do you need to bear in mind how the method of teaching corresponds to what is being taught. For example, if you decide that all the children in your class would benefit from some exercises in colour mixing you may decide that a whole class lesson would be appropriate, during which you would demonstrate how to mix colours and give advice about handling the brush, keeping the powder paint dry and so on. In contrast, if you decide that one or two children need to talk further about problems in their work, you may need to find a time when the rest of the class is busily occupied and then sit with the children for a structured conversation, in which case your teaching role will be very different from the colour mixing lesson. The National Curriculum for art states that children should be given the opportunity to work as individuals, in groups or as a whole class, and this scheme will give you the opportunity to plan appropriately for this.

For those of you committed to giving children maximum opportunity to plan their own learning, the scheme can be formulated after an initial discussion with the class. For example, within an already planned whole school curriculum scheme based on given topics, there is still room for individual or class decisions about the direction and content of the work.

The overall aims in an art scheme should broadly correspond to the National Curriculum attainment targets, and the learning outcomes should express the number of learning objectives for each lesson. The schemes of work which follow offer a model that can facilitate the planning of broad aims, with learning outcomes and brief descriptions given for each lesson. We have built into this model an opportunity for groups to talk with their teacher after the third lesson, and evaluate the work so far, in the context of an impromptu display of their work. Also built in is an opportunity for a whole class display at the end of the scheme of lessons which will act both as a celebration of the work and as an interactive opportunity for summative assessment. Included are opportunities for support/extension exercises.

The lesson plan includes an introduction to the lesson, its development and conclusion. There is also a space to comment on the proposed time the lesson might take, the type of formative assessment a teacher might make with the class and any support or extension exercises the pupils might need to develop further their ideas and experience.

In the examples that follow there are two termly schemes and two half-termly schemes, each with a particular emphasis but including reference to both attainment targets.

- *Scheme 1 (a term's work)* Investigating and making – the development of three-dimensional form and structure.
- *Scheme 2 (half a term's work)* Investigating and making – drawing the figure.
- *Scheme 3 (half a term's work)* Investigating and making – the element of pattern.
- *Scheme 4 (a term's work)* Knowledge and understanding – critical studies through thematic work based on reproductions of Impressionist works of art.

It is important to note that the lessons are offered as sample lessons that would be appropriate in a broad sense for key stage 2 but would need to be adapted to suit the needs of particular classes. Each of the lessons may need to be adapted or extended for the children you teach, depending on their past experience, their ability and their particular needs.

Scheme 1

Scheme 1 (Figure 6.3) concentrates on three-dimensional work in pottery and sculpture. This is an area that is potentially enriching for primary pupils, but one which many primary teachers feel a lack of confidence in teaching. It is beyond the scope of this book to give a complete overview of ceramics teaching but the scheme will enable teachers to find out what they need to research so that they can teach the lessons effectively. The scheme and lesson notes do not concern themselves with the technical matters of making, firing, decorating and glazing because it is assumed that if a school is equipped for ceramics then a teacher will already have the necessary technical knowledge. However, it is perfectly feasible to carry out this scheme with self-hardening clay which requires no technical knowledge. This clay will harden after making and can then be coated with PVA adhesive and painted, if necessary, with water-based colour. With most relief work and sculpture the three-dimensional forms that the children make can be ruined by brightly coloured painting, which will counteract the subtle effects of light and shadow. It might be better to colour the surface by spraying or painting with one or two more neutral colours, or by polishing the surface with shoe cream.

If teachers do wish to develop their skills in teaching ceramics it might be a good idea to work alongside a teacher more confident in using clay or to invest in some good books on clay work, as well as asking the local advisory teacher or advisor for art for some support. However many the difficulties may be, we feel sure that one of the best ways to learn about the medium is to work alongside the children and learn with them. Children enjoy working with a teacher in this co-operative way and sharing the successes and pitfalls accordingly.

After the scheme and the lessons, further advice is offered so that teachers can approach the activities that follow with confidence.

The first three lessons of this scheme have been worked out, and hopefully the method is clear and in sufficient detail for the lessons to be taught. The emphasis is not on pottery but on using clay as a modelling material for sculpture and relief sculpture, related to the analysis of forms and structure.

Although lesson 4 is to do with making a cylindrical slab pot, its principle aim is to develop the idea of the relief imagery covered in lesson 3, by changing the relief into silhouette form and treating it in a more decorative way using shapes, spaces and lines. This could be done using paper, brush and ink, or cut silhouette work which would also relate

[*text continues on page 103*]

Figure 6.2 Scheme of work for art 1: three-dimensional work

SCHEME OF WORK FOR ART 1: three-dimensional work

Aims: To develop observational work into imaginative three-dimensional sculpture and pottery through a variety of materials appropriate to the child's intention, imagery, and the function of artefact.

Learning Outcomes: (a) Learning how to choose materials, methods and visual elements appropriate for making images and artefacts for different purposes. (b) Recording what has been experienced and imagined. (c) Expressing ideas and feelings. (d) Increasing powers of looking and seeing through close observation. (e) Experimenting with ideas generated by materials. (f) Learning from relevant works of art to enhance children's work.

....

Lesson 1 'Understanding organic forms and structures' – drawing and clay modelling from observation – whole/sections of fruit and vegetables. Refer to Henry Moore's drawings and sculpture.
Support/extension exercise Cut a section through an orange, cabbage or apple and make a large chalk drawing, concentrating on its internal structure.

....

Lesson 2 'Imaginative development of form' – developing drawings of vegetables. Clay sculpture – create magical creature using forms and surfaces of vegetables as inspiration. Include a narrative input. Refer to the ceramics of Alan Barrett-Danes/Star Wars-type illustrations.
Support/extension exercise In sketch books, children write and draw five important things about the character and habits of their creature and give it a name.

....

Lesson 3 'Tile making in clay' – create a magical creature, using relief form and texture. Refer to medieval relief carving/Chinese dragon/insects, beetles.
Support/extension exercise Take rubbings of different surfaces, mount in sketch books.

....

Lesson 4 'Cylindrical slab pot' (at least 30cm high), decorative relief frieze around pot of magical creature and family. Refer to Greek art/Red and Black figure pots.
Support/extension exercise Draw in sketch book from Greek frieze/pot hand-out.

Impromptu display ↔ class/group formative assessment

....

Lessons 5 and 6 'Create sculptural modelled heads in clay' of magical creatures (at least 40cm tall) based on drawings, illustrations and source material; put emphasis on formal structure – concentration on scales, hair, armour, jewellery, crowns, etc. Refer to gargoyles, Hieronymus Bosch fantasy creatures, Star Wars characters.
Support/extension exercise Collect images of medieval gargoyles, space creatures, dragons, etc. and mount in sketch books.

....

Lesson 7 'Investigate manufactured form' – drawings from observation of household objects with mechanistic forms: cheese graters, tin-opener, garlic press, cog-wheels, etc.
Support/extension exercise Collect photographs, illustrations of aggressive looking mechanical objects and mount in sketch books.

....

Lesson 8 'Construct a relief panel in card' based on shapes derived from drawings of mechanical objects. Refer to Claes Oldenburg's drawings/Cubist constructions.
Support/extension exercise Design a standing sculpture entitled 'Fantastic building'.

....

Lesson 9 Construct a standing sculpture, 'Tower'; concentrate on form, space and surface – based on previous drawings and collected photographs, using card, corroflute, etc. Refer to the sculptors Reg Butler, Eduardo Paolozzi, Jean Tinguely, the pottery of Brian Newman, medieval paintings of the Tower of Babel.

Support/extension exercise Make drawings in sketch books of scaffolding, collect magazine cuttings, illustrations of pylons, bridges, and modern buildings.

Lessons 10, 11, 12 'Construct a life-sized figure' using card and collage material; group work based on the 'shopper', ' soldier', ' motorcyclist', 'parent with pram', 'tramp' . Collect contextual material – information, drawings, photographs. Refer to Picasso's constructed sculpture (Mother with pram, Goat, etc.), Duane Hanson (American tourists/Motorcyclists), Eduardo Paolozzi (Japanese War God, etc.)

Whole class display ↔ *individual/group summative assessment*

Figure 6.2 continued

LESSON PLANNING SHEET 1

Aim: Recording from observation through modelling and drawing. **Date** _____ **Class** _____
Learning Outcomes: Developing an understanding and making representation of natural forms.
Whole class . . .   Group (6 groups of 5 pupils) . . .   Individuals . . .   Duration afternoon/2 hours
(could be expanded into two lessons)

Introduction
Teacher Set up fruit and vegetables on each table – cabbage, onion, apples, oranges, potatoes –
together with interesting pebbles/shells/flints. Introduce idea of 3-D form and how it differs from flat
shape. Discuss surface texture. Demonstrate modelling from observation and how an apple might be
made from a 'ball' of clay whereas a cabbage might need some overlapping leaves. Point out how
texture of leaves might be imprinted into clay. Give out equipment.
Pupil Model chosen (vegetable/pebble, etc.) from observation. Think about its form and how to make
it – moulding in hands, rolling like a ball, beating into shape with wood, etc. Think about surface
texture.
Resources Clay, vegetables/pebbles/shells/bones, modelling boards, tools, variety of textural
objects to press into clay surface, water, sponges, aprons, newspapers.

Development
Teacher Clear away clay, retain models and distribute new materials for drawing. Recap ideas of
volume and surface, refer to vegetables, etc. and demonstrate how the modelled objects can be
represented in drawing by using light and shade (directional light from window or light source useful).
Use appropriate vocabulary to describe form and surfaces – rounded, knobby, smooth, rough, etc.
Pupil Make large drawings using charcoal and chalk on grey paper, refer to vegetables/stones/shells
and their models of vegetables/stones/shells.
Resources Grey sugar paper, charcoal, chalk , pebbles, stones, etc.

Conclusion
Teacher and Pupil Class discussion, compare the drawings and models. Discuss the different ways
they represent what has been observed. Point out ideas of volume, form, surface and texture.
Discuss light and shade, and how this can be used to convey an illusion of three dimensions on a
two-dimensional surface. Compare work with drawings and sculpture by Henry Moore.
Resources Children's drawings and models with reproductions of Henry Moore's work.

Formative assessment As above
Support/extension exercise Cut a section through oranges, cabbages and apples. Make a second
large chalk drawing concentrating on internal structure.

LESSON PLANNING SHEET 2

Aim Express imaginative ideas through sculptural form.   **Date** _____ **Class** _____
Learning outcomes Relating previous experience of observational work to development of imaginative ideas; develop appropriate visual elements to convey ideas through modelling; looking at work of artists to identify similarities and differences and to inform own work.
Whole class . . .   Group . . .   Individuals . . .   Duration afternoon/2 hours

....

Introduction
Teacher Recap the qualities of form and texture developed by the children in last lesson. Talk to children about artists who have used similar forms and textures to make pictures/sculptures of magical creatures. Pictures referring to medieval dragons, ceramic sculpture of Alan Barrett-Danes, Star Wars figures, Water World creatures, etc. Discuss how children will make a large clay sculpture using ideas of surface, form or texture developed through work on vegetables.
Pupil Talk about resource material and artists' work in small groups and respond to teacher's questions.
Resources Pictures, children's previous work.

....

Development
Teacher Give out materials. Demonstrate ways of making sculpture employing techniques (modelling, rolling, slabbing, surface texture printing) and qualities of form (round, angular, etc.) developed in last lesson. Refer to pictures as above and discuss characteristics/habits of magical creatures (aggressive, fearsome, sly, flying, crawling, etc.) Standing creatures are difficult, suggest a lying down/sitting pose.
Pupil Brainstorm five minutes – write down ideas about magical creature. Model creature in clay concentrating on body shape, surface detail and the addition of human or reptile features (hair, eyes, wings, tail, spikes, teeth, etc.)
Resources Paper, pencils, pictures, postcards, posters, etc.; clay, tools, found objects such as screws, nuts, bolts, netting, etc. for surface texture.

....

Conclusion
Teacher and Pupil Display sculptures as a group on different levels, assembling as children finish. Talk about learning outcomes, encourage children to talk about the character of their creature.
Resources Table area, sugar paper, felt-tip pens for labelling.

....

Formative assessment Peer/teacher evaluation as above.
Support/extension exercise In sketch books, children draw and write five important things about their creature, how it looks, what it does, what its family is like, its name, etc.

Figure 6.2 continued

LESSON PLANNING SHEET 3

Aim: To develop imaginatively previous work and extend it   **Date** _____ **Class** _____
through relief modelling.
Learning outcomes: To reflect and adapt previous work, identifying ways it can be developed; to
employ formal and surface elements to convey an idea through an image; to compare images
including work of artists, using art, craft and design vocabulary.
Whole class . . .   Group . . .   Individuals . . .   Duration 2/hours
....

Introduction
Teacher Introduce pupils to characteristics of relief sculpture. Refer to posters, photographs,
drawings of carved figures and decoration in church architecture, memorials, gravestones. Point out
relief decoration around school, e.g. drain covers, memorial plaques, embossed lettering, etc.
Discuss surface quality, e.g. contrasts between pattern/plain areas, rough/smooth surfaces, deep
shadows in indentations. Give clay to children. Simple demonstration, referring to pictures: (a)
Rolling out clay slabs; (b) impressing pattern into clay using tools, found objects, textured materials,
etc.; (c) surface patterns and textures using coils, balls, cut-out shapes and imprinting.
Pupil After teacher introduction and demonstration, children experiment and respond to each idea,
making their own version of pattern, surface texture, etc.
Resources Pictures, posters, clay, tools, found objects (screws, nuts, bolts, etc.) for surface texture.
....

Development
Teacher Outline design brief for relief sculpture on tile (30cm square, round). Creatures can now fly,
leap, spring across surface. Monitor work, supporting and extending children's ideas and outcomes.
Pupil Brainstorm on paper ideas about magical creature. Refer back to previous sculpture and
extend its features to develop new expressive work on tiles. Discuss with teacher ideas about relief
sculpture, pattern, shadow, etc.
Resources Paper, pencil, cardboard templates for tile shapes.
....

Conclusion
Teacher Display relief tiles in directional light, point out light and shadow, and qualities related to
relief forms and surfaces.
Pupil Peer evaluation of own and others' work, relating to original visual stimulus.
Resources Display area for work.
....

Formative assessment Peer/teacher evaluation as above.
Support/extension exercise Taking rubbings from different surfaces, mount in sketch books.

the children's work to images from Ancient Greece. This image could then be transferred to the pot.

The second part of the scheme, after lesson 7, changes the emphasis from working with organic forms to working with more geometric ones. It also changes the emphasis from modelling to constructing using card, glue-guns, wire, corroflute and more rigid materials. The structure of lessons 7 to 12 broadly repeat the pattern of lessons 1 to 6, moving from investigation of observed objects to imaginative images made in relief and full three-dimensional sculpture. Also, like the first half of the scheme, it seeks to relate to attainment targets 1 and 2 in all lessons.

    ## TEACHER ACTIVITY 6.2

Working with some colleagues, construct a series of lessons based on the above scheme from lesson 7 to lesson 12. This will involve some research into the work of modern sculptors and potters. The artists mentioned mostly appear with illustrations of their work in any general history of modern sculpture. Many good videotapes are now available which not only provide examples of artists' work but also a commentary, which will enable teachers to initiate discussion about key issues and images with the children (see 'Resources for art teaching', page 131).

When the first draft of the lessons is complete consult other colleagues about the practicality of resourcing the scheme with materials and equipment. The consumable materials should be obtainable with hardly any cost; however, good 'fixing' materials and equipment are important, so glue-guns, adhesives, tapes and staples will need to be budgeted for in the school's planning.

Scheme 2

This scheme (Figure 6.4) might fit directly into the term planning in the last Unit, 'Ourselves' (Figure 5.2, page 77). From a very early age, children like Joseph and Lorna (page 52) are fascinated by the human form and it is often one of their earliest representations. In scheme 2 emphasis is given to developing children's understanding of the human form through the opportunity to look closely at bodies, their own and others, and to learn also by looking at the drawings made by artists about the figure. Any of the approaches through drawing described in these lessons could be repeated with painting as the activity, with an extension to looking at painting as well as drawings. Most libraries will have books on the artists given as examples, but other artists' work, whose drawing shows evidence of line and form, could be used instead.

The three sample lessons provided in Figure 6.4 have been written with enough detail to help a non-specialist primary teacher plan and teach a similar lesson. You will see that the scheme has been devised so that the skills in handling materials are put in place before the children are asked to draw from observation. The children may in fact need much longer than one lesson to learn sufficient skills in handling pencil and charcoal – it is a lifetime's learning process for many artists. However, as a class teacher you will be in a
[*text continues on page 108*]

Figure 6.3 Scheme of work for art 2: drawing the figure

SCHEME OF WORK FOR ART 2: drawing the figure

Aims: To help children represent chosen features (figure) of the world around them with increased accuracy and attention to detail. To reflect on and adapt their work, identifying ways it can be developed and improved. Look at work of artists to identify similarities and differences. AT1 and AT2.
Learning outcomes: (a) Increased powers of looking and seeing through close observation. (b) Developed understanding/use of line, shape, form, colour. (c) Increased skill at handling media. (d) Increased ability to appraise own and other artists' work.

....

Lesson 1 Introduction to scheme: preparatory exercises in pencil use and control – line.
Support/extension exercise 'Take a line for a walk' exercise for homework.

....

Lesson 2 Drawing part of somebody else – select detail, e.g. eye, finger, ear. Large-scale, A4 drawings from observation using a range of pencils (2B to 6B).
Support/extension exercise Children collect photographs, magazine cuttings of bodies for sketch books.

....

Lesson 3 A4 pattern and tone exercises in charcoal use and control. Look at the drawings of Leonardo, Rembrandt, Van Gogh, Kathe Kollwitz.
Support/extension exercise Children find books, postcards, magazine cuttings of artists' work on the figure.

Impromptu display ↔ *class/group, formative assessment*

....

Lesson 4 Drawing the head of a friend – observational drawing concentrating on form, shape, proportion, detail using choice of pencil or charcoal.
Support/extension exercise Drawings in sketch books of hair detail from family at home.

....

Lesson 5 Introducing colour – exercises in using pastels. Look at the work of Modigliani, Giacometti, Picasso to study subject, composition and background, line, colour, form.
Support/extension exercise Drawings in sketch book of family at home.

....

Lesson 6 Pastel observational drawings of figure in context – A3 size.

Whole class display ↔ *individual/group, summative assessment*

Figure 6.3 continued

LESSON PLANNING SHEET 1

Aim: To build children's confidence in using drawing pencils.   **Date** _____ **Class** _____
Learning outcomes: An increased understanding of the potential of a range of drawing pencils in creating a full range of marks.
Whole class . . .   Group . . .   Individuals . . .   Duration 2 hours
(may extend to two lessons)

Introduction
Teacher Introduce the scheme, identifying the purpose of the lessons for both ATs. Talk about the need to be proficient in handling materials (i.e. pencils) in order to produce drawings with interesting range of marks, concentrating firstly on 'line' exercises. Demonstrate first exercise – draw a rough grid of squares on A4 paper and fill each square with different marks (tone, pattern, expressive marks).
Pupil Talk about previous experience of drawing with pencil and problems they may have encountered. Do exercise 1 – exploring the range of marks, patterns, tones from pencils 2B to 6B.
Resources Newspaper on tables. Pencils 2B to 6B, A4 cartridge paper, rulers.

Development
Teacher Move around the class talking to individual and groups about the work. Extend to exercise 2 – line exercise to gain idea of pattern from line and greater pencil control.
Pupil Exercise 2: On A4 paper pupils draw three triangles spaced out. They then draw a line, freehand, from one edge of the paper to the other, carefully drawing lines parallel to the edges of the triangles when they meet one. Pupils continue lines until surface is filled with line pattern, taking own time to complete.
Resources As above plus wall space for children to mount work quickly as a group 'patchwork'.

Conclusion
Teacher As a whole class, look at the range of marks produced. Ask children to identify what they have learned about the potential of the pencils, and the creation of tone and pattern from line.
Pupil Discuss with each other and with teacher their learning about line, tone, pattern. Take down work, mount selection in sketch books and write brief comments.
Resources Sketch books, glue, dictionaries.

Formative assessment Discussion with groups and class about learning.
Support/extension exercise 'Take a line for a walk' exercise as homework in sketch book in which pupils make further pattern as in exercise 2, but draw circles and ovals instead of triangles – a very different pattern will form.

Figure 6.3 continued

LESSON PLANNING SHEET 2

Aim: Develop observation skills through drawing figure detail, large scale.

Date _____ **Class** _____

Learning outcomes: Understanding of process of planning a drawing; scale and proportion; detail through mark making.

Whole class . . .   Group . . .   Individuals . . .   Duration 2 hours

....

Introduction

Teacher Talk with children about purpose of lesson. Emphasise that they will be drawing part of a body much bigger than it is. In order to give room for detail they will be 'scaling up' freehand (without need to use grid as in design work).

Pupil Look back at work from last lesson to recall how certain marks were made with which pencils. Choose detail to be drawn and tell partner about what can be seen.

Resources Children's previous work.

....

Development

Teacher Demonstrate how to scale up drawing of a detail. Provide materials, ask children to choose partner or work individually.

Pupil Choose partner and select part, e.g. eye, to be drawn from observation. Sit so that the part can be observed closely. Sketch in lightly to place drawing on paper. Pay close attention to detail of tone, pattern, texture. Draw this using variety of pencils.

Resources Magnifying glasses, A4 paper, pencils 2B to 6B.

....

Conclusion

Teacher Divide class up into groups of four and ask pupils to discuss observed detail. Point out positive attributes of individual work, drawing attention to scale, proportion, detail, mark making.

Pupil Say what they like about their own and others' work, why they like it (scale, detail, etc.), and what might be improved.

Resources Wall space for quick display.

....

Formative assessment Peer evaluation with teacher input as above.

Support/extension exercise Children select from school/home resources, magazine cuttings, photographs of detail of human form. Mount for wall display or in sketch books.

Figure 6.3 continued

LESSON PLANNING SHEET 3

Aim: To build children's confidence/ability in using charcoal.   **Date** _____ **Class** _____
Learning outcomes: Increased awareness of the potential of charcoal's expressive qualities.
Whole class . . .   Group . . .   Individuals . . .   Duration 2 hours

Introduction
Teacher Recap on lesson 1 to remind children of the quality of mark making achieved in pencil exercises. Introduce charcoal as new medium, give to children for free experiment on large sheets of paper. Set time limit of ten minutes. Ask children to find out all about mark making using charcoal.
Pupil Experiment making variety of different marks with charcoal.
Resources Newspaper on tables, aprons on children, A3 paper, hair spray for fixing drawings when children are gone.

Development
Teacher Bring drawing experiment to a close. Ask children to view each other's work and to talk about the variety and quality of marks (smudged, misty, angry, criss-crossed, messy, sharp, soft, etc.) List on board as children respond. Give children clean A3 paper and ask them to draw a continuous looping line from one corner to the diagonal corner. Ask them to fill, with care, the enclosed shapes they have created with as wide a variety of marks, patterns and tones as they can think of. Show them how to avoid smudging the work by laying a clean piece of paper over the work on which to rest hand.
Pupil Respond to above exercises, making and extending mark making in as many ways as they can, borrowing ideas from each other. Extend their vocabulary of elements – line, tone, patterns and texture.
Resources A3 paper, charcoal.

Conclusion
Teacher and pupil Lay out children's work, ask children to discuss nature and qualities that they like/dislike in the work. Show them other artists' drawings. Ask them to identify which are pencil or charcoal and encourage them to make connections between their work and that of the artists, emphasising appreciation of quality of marks.
Resources Children's and artists' drawings.

Formative assessment Peer/teacher evaluation as above, based around display of children's work and contextual studies.
Support/extension exercise Children select favourite section of one artist's drawing. Make an enlarged photocopy for the children to 'copy' in their sketch books.

good position to know your children's previous experience in handling various drawing materials and will be able to gauge how much practice individuals will need.

It is important to ensure that the children are confident in using the pencil or charcoal before you ask them to draw from observation, so that they can anticipate which sort of marks will be appropriate when making their drawing of an eye or a section of hair. If they feel familiar with the medium and confident in using it they will be able to give greater attention to the many difficult problems confronting them in drawing from observation – problems like scale, proportion, detail, how to portray a textural surface or the rounded form of an arm or elbow. The drawings in Figure 6.4 by a Year 6 class show the children posing for each other and confronting the challenges with energy, achieving a good sense of a sitting figure with the weight on one arm, as well as some interesting pattern and marks.

Drawing from observation is challenging for children and adults alike and as the children's teacher you will be needed to support, encourage, and point out areas that might be improved. Sometimes, if you feel able, you can talk children through a problem and do a demonstration drawing on your own piece of paper to show what you mean. You don't have to be good at drawing in order to do this, but it can be very helpful for children to see how a few lines in the right place can suggest a solution to a problem.

If you do not feel able to draw in this way, start a collection of photocopies and postcards of artists' drawings as a visual resource file for children to use. Many artists, as they cannot have a model to hand all the time, use such a resource when they need a ready reference for drawing a figure in a particular attitude.

Bearing in mind the need to support children, scheme 2 has suggested that it will help if children draw small parts of the body before attempting the whole! Again, your children may need to have extra lessons drawing feet, hands, and so on before going on to tackle a whole figure. When you do get to lesson 6, however, you and the children can have some fun setting the figure in any context you like. It might be that you invite a parent into school and ask them to pose in a swimming costume in a deck chair, as if on a beach. The children can then have fun painting a background, either to have it ready to set the figure on, or to add afterwards.

You might get the children to pose for each other as characters from history, as in the drawings in Figure 6.5, as Victorians or Greeks, perhaps, or as the characters in a famous painting. You might even offer yourself as a model.

Lesson 6 requires you to introduce children to the work of artists. As with any other lesson preparation, it is wise to acquaint yourself with details about the artists before the lesson so that you are in an informed position to answer the children's questions. Any research you do may be useful for other members of staff, and some schools are beginning a resource file about artists for children and staff to use.

In the following activity you are asked to complete the planning for lessons 4, 5 and 6, ensuring that your plan is in similar detail and takes into account the aims of the National Curriculum for art.

 TEACHER ACTIVITY 6.3

Working with the art co-ordinator, read the scheme and the first three lessons

Figure 6.4 Drawings of the figure

Figure 6.5 Drawings of two characters from history

carefully. Brainstorm each lesson and then refine your ideas so that they represent a realistic lesson with appropriate learning objectives for the children. Try to achieve a balance between practical making activities and opportunities for the children to learn from looking at art. The model of peer/teacher evaluation suggested in the sample lesson seems to us to present a workable assessment procedure, with display providing a focus of the children's work and contextual studies in lesson 3. In planning for the summative assessment in or after lesson 6, you may wish to consider a realistic way of recording your views, and the children's views, of their learning in a manner used by your school.

When you have drafted the remaining lessons consult with other colleagues to see if your planning has taken into account the particular nature of your school, its policy statement for art and the requirements of the National Curriculum.

Scheme 3

Scheme 3 (Figure 6.7) concentrates on pattern, one of the most exciting and enjoyable elements of art to introduce to children. Most young children pattern naturally. It seems that they enjoy filling spaces with repeated patterns and that they also enjoy developing sequences of pattern, gradually extending the number in the sequences as they mature, developing mathematical as well as visual skills. Victoria's drawings of 'ladies' (page 56) and
[*text continues on page 116*]

Figure 6.6 Scheme of work for art 3: pattern

SCHEME OF WORK FOR ART 3: pattern

Aims: Record what they have experienced and imagined, expressing ideas and feelings confidently. Represent chosen features of the world around them with increasing accuracy and attention to detail. Select relevant resources and materials, and use methods and visual elements (pattern) appropriate to their intentions. Reflect on and adapt their work, identifying ways it can be developed and improved. Identify similarities and differences in methods in work of artists. AT1 and AT2.

Learning outcomes: (a) To open up awareness of the element of pattern in the natural and made world. (b) To learn investigative and research skills in relation to art. (c) To experiment and use a range of materials to make patterns. (d) To investigate the work of artists for whom pattern is an important element. (e) To be aware of the use of a sketch book in the processes of art making.

....

Lesson 1 Introduce children to scheme. Give out new sketch books especially for work on pattern. Talk about natural and made pattern, showing examples from photographs, magazine cuttings, books. Divide children into groups and send them off to make rubbings of natural and made patterned surfaces in classroom, school and playground. Further, draw patterns and photograph them.
Support/extension exercise Children begin collecting magazine cuttings of pattern, mount in sketch books and write about them.

....

Lesson 2 Look at rubbings from lesson 1 and discuss different patterns. Look at photographs of rubbings. Plan a display for rubbings and photographs. Children select a sample for their folders. Children make a pattern collage from remaining rubbings, concentrating on either 'geometrical' pattern cutting with scissors or 'organic' patterns, tearing paper with their fingers.
Support/extension exercise Children with cameras at home photograph patterns for the display. Children without cameras make further rubbings using gold/silver crayons.

....

Lesson 3 Choosing one rubbing they like, children use it as a basis for designing a pattern using wax resist process (wax crayons and coloured inks).
Support/extension exercise Children experiment with art IT programmes to make patterns.

Impromptu display ↔ class/group formative assessment

....

Lesson 4 Individual children design wrapping paper using IT art programme that allows for repetition of an image. Print out designs. Other children plan and make material collages based on pattern, exploring the nature and qualities of different materials.
Support/extension exercise Children collect and mount samples of patterned materials in sketch books, writing about the possible use of samples in fashion/household design.

....

Lesson 5 Pattern in line using felt-tips on coloured sugar paper, children draw round hand or scissors on paper five times, changing position each time to create overlap. They fill in spaces with as many different patterns made from lines as they can. Mount work as class 'patchwork'. Look at work of Bridget Riley and Paul Klee, exploring use of line in artists' work.

Figure 6.6 continued

LESSON PLANNING SHEET 2

AIM: To reinforce the notion of pattern element through further   **Date** _____ **Class** _____
looking. To create in collage a pattern from selected samples, concentrating on repetition of marks, colour, shape.
Learning outcomes: To use increased understanding of pattern as an element. To create a collage pattern.
Whole class . . .   Group . . .   Individuals . . .   Duration 2 hours
....

Introduction
Teacher Look at photographs, drawings and rubbings made in last lesson and select a sample for wall display and art folders. Plan display with pupils.
Pupil Talk about patterns, classifying into natural and made, regular and irregular. Plan wall display, sorting out backing paper, labels, etc.
Resources Rubbings, photographs, drawings.
....

Development
Teacher Introduce children to the idea of making a collage by selecting from remaining rubbings interesting shapes, colours, marks that can be cut and torn and rearranged to make a new pattern. Talk about how the pattern might be regular with repeated shapes and colours, or irregular with certain shapes and colours repeated randomly. Give a demonstration of how the collage will look different when: (a) the pieces are cut with scissors and arranged to give a geometrical pattern; (b) the pieces are torn with the fingers to give a softer edged, more organic look. Point out the need for contrast in work. Remind children to take time arranging their collages in a satisfactory way before sticking them down.
Pupil Select a number of rubbings and look carefully at patterns. Cut or tear into sections/shapes and rearrange until the new pattern is satisfactory. After sticking down the pieces onto a base piece of paper, mount on sympathetic coloured sugar paper.
Resources Papers, rubbings, glue, spreaders, aprons, scissors.
....

Conclusion
Teacher and Pupil Lay out the collages and look at the variety produced. Look at the similarities and differences. Ask individuals if there is any way they might have been improved. Decide on how to display on wall, label and display.
Resources Wall boards, papers, art work, etc.
....

Formative assessment Peer/teacher evaluations as above.
Support/extension exercise Children with cameras at home photograph patterns for display; other children make further rubbings with gold and silver crayons.

Figure 6.6 continued

LESSON PLANNING SHEET 3

Aim: To select relevant resources and materials, and use   **Date** _____ **Class** _____
methods and visual elements appropriate to their intentions.
Learning outcomes: Developing an ability to select materials, resources and methods to make a
new image.
Whole class ...   Group ...   Individuals ...   Duration 2 hours
....

Introduction
Teacher Introduce the children to the wax resist process through demonstration using wax crayons
and coloured inks. Talk about how they can select a part of one of the rubbings they like and use this
section as a starting point for a large pattern by either: (a) copying the section onto the paper and
extending the lines, colours, marks, shapes away from the section in a pattern until the paper is filled;
or (b) repeating the section again and again in different sizes and colours until the paper is filled.
Show children how to make a small paper 'window' to lay on the rubbing in order to identify clearly
their section of pattern. Give out A3 paper, inks, aprons.
Pupil Select a part of a rubbing they like using the window and decide how to go about making their
large pattern. Experiment with wax crayons and inks in sketch books or on paper if necessary.
Resources A3 paper, crayons, inks, aprons, windows, newspaper on tables. Drying rack.
....

Development
Teacher Monitor children's work, giving support and advice to individuals, groups, class when
appropriate. Enforce rules about handling of inks.
Pupil Create large pattern concentrating on repeated pattern, regular and irregular pattern, with
colour adding to pattern element.
Resources As above.
....

Conclusion
Teacher and pupil Lay out work on tables. Discuss similarities and differences. Discuss success of
handling materials and creation of new patterns. Discuss how to mount when dry. Place on drying
rack.
....

Display class/teacher formative assessment
Support/extension exercise Children experiment with art IT programmes that allow for repetition of
images.

the mosaics (Plate 12) are good examples of enjoyment of patterning. This desire to decorate the surfaces of pictures, the objects we make and the clothes we wear, in a way that we find aesthetically pleasing, is evident across all cultures, in all ages.

In the next teacher activity you are asked to write the next three lessons for this work on pattern. Children following this scheme will come to appreciate the important part pattern plays in enriching their lives. You may like to consider extending the work into music, where pattern also has a vital role to play, and to English where pattern in words is celebrated in poetry. In writing the lessons bear in mind that the children in your class will have much to contribute in telling you about the visual element of pattern in their lives. Pattern can also link the children to other cultures who value pattern highly. For example, they could be introduced to the rich surface patterns of Indian miniature paintings; the mathematical patterns in Islamic design; Mendhi hand patterns worn by Muslim women and children on special celebratory occasions; and appliqué patterns from India and North American Indian designs. Making such global links will enable children to see their part in appreciating and creating pattern. Plates 13 and 14 are examples of work from other cultures used as a stimulus for primary children's work.

 TEACHER ACTIVITY 6.4

Working with the art co-ordinator, brainstorm and plan for the next three lessons. Decide if you wish to enrich the children's experience by building in a trip to the local museum or a trip to a London museum or gallery (the Museum of Mankind, for example) in order to examine patterned artefacts first-hand. You may wish to put part of the school budget aside for developing a resource box for pattern containing a variety of richly patterned artefacts from Britain and elsewhere. This resource could be used in conjunction with the scheme and particularly in lesson 5 when you could extend looking at the work of artists to include craft and design.

When you are happy with the lessons, show them to other members of staff to see if you are meeting the needs of the children and the school.

Scheme 4

The following scheme for critical studies work (Figure 6.8) is broadly aimed at Years 5 and 6 pupils, but could be adapted to suit younger children. This is a key area of interest within this book, and building up the knowledge and experience to deal with this scheme has been covered in the previous Units. Each lesson in the scheme starts with some kind of analysis of pictures. This corresponds to attainment target 2 of the National Curriculum. Each lesson also links what has been learned by this analysis to children's own practical work through investigating sources and making images. Consequently, both attainment targets are linked and most lessons are also two hours long, so they could carry on over a two-week cycle or take place twice in one week.

This means that you will need to recap the previous lesson at the start of the next; this is indicated in the sample lesson notes.

Historical and critical studies need to be focused on a historical period. This scheme takes its examples from French Impressionism and relates to Unit 2 and 5, in which it was suggested that people, their immediate environment and the broader environment were suitable starting points. In this scheme, people are dealt with through the art form of portraits. The immediate environment is dealt with through still life and the broader environment is dealt with through landscape. Portrait, still life and landscape are the main forms of painting to have developed historically in Europe.

It will be apparent that this scheme has resource implications. Most schools are not overly endowed with reproductions of paintings, slides, videotapes, and art history books, but will need to invest in some of these materials to teach art effectively within the requirements of the National Curriculum. Much can be done by collecting thematic sets of A4 reproductions, thematic books or CD-ROMs (see 'Resources for art teaching', page 135). Many books with good reproductions are now available at a low price, and can be used in their own right or taken apart to make work cards or example sheets. Most of the lessons suggest that children should work individually, whilst in groups. This is important for two reasons – first because small resource packs are more easily devised, and second, and of more importance, because talking and writing about works of art is one of the best ways of learning about them. Group discussion and presentation enable children to share and communicate their ideas. Display in this situation needs to be an integral part of the programme, providing stimulus, resources, and a developing record and celebration of the children's work (Plate 15).

Most lessons start with worksheets. These are effective in group work and can provide variety within the same lesson. They relate to topics such as formal elements, painting techniques and reading pictures at a variety of different levels. The scheme also suggests a museum visit and exhibitions of contextual work, in order to make critical studies come alive and to relate it to first-hand experiences of interrogating real pictures and artefacts.

 TEACHER ACTIVITY 6.6

After a preliminary visit to a gallery, devise a worksheet. You should be able to incorporate some ideas from the worksheets in the resources section (pages 132–4), which have been devised by student teachers. Think how you might enable the children to 'discover' the particular paintings you have previously researched. Think of which paintings would be suitable for demonstrating certain features, perhaps a particular mood, or the use of formal elements, or the way the paint has been applied. You might wish to ask the children to identify certain historical features, such as particular objects or costumes which might relate to your topic or a contextual display.

A gallery visit should provide the opportunity for what Rod Taylor (1986) calls an 'illuminating experience', indicating personal selection on the part of the pupil which might reflect something within their past or initiate some spark which opens the door to new experiences. The worksheet will need to relate to work in the

[text continues on page 123]

Figure 6.7 Scheme of work for art 4: critical studies

SCHEME OF WORK FOR ART 4: critical studies

Aims: To engage children actively in the critical study of painting in order to enhance their visual literacy and picture making.

Learning outcomes: (a) To encourage children to compare images using art, craft and design vocabulary, and recognise similarities and differences in various types of art. (b) To identify the elements of visual literacy in work of established artists. (c)To talk about and understand the content of pictures and their historical context. (d) To reflect on and adapt their work, identifying ways it can be developed and improved by reference to work of artists. (e) To evaluate their own and others work in the light of what was intended.

....

Lesson 1 Introduce scheme – explain how we can learn about art by looking at artists' work. Teacher-led class discussion of different art forms. Class activity identifying similarities and differences between examples distributed to groups. Children sort examples into categories of art, craft and design, make notes in sketch books and assemble into group displays.
Support/extension exercise Mount in sketch book an example of painting, sculpture, photograph, a craft object, example of design.

....

Lessons 2/3 Investigate similarities between portraits, still life and landscape. Group work classifying and sorting using either postcards, CD-ROM gallery programme, or videodisc gallery programme. Whole class drawing still life, portraits or views through window.
Support/extension exercise Children collect magazine cuttings of portraits and landscapes, and mount in sketch books.

Display ↔ class/group formative assessment

....

Lessons 4/5 Analysing painting technique – give groups reproductions of artists' paintings (or CD-ROM videodisc), using worksheets for children to analyse (a) how paint has been used to make particular effects, and (b) what types of brushstrokes have been used. Children carry out painting exercises from worksheets based on the reproductions. Children paint landscapes from window or from school playground, employing paint quality and brushstrokes they have practised.
Support/extension exercise Pastel drawings of trees in sketch books, employing a range of marks.

....

Lessons 6/7 Analysing formal elements (line, shape, colour, form, pattern, texture, etc.) in six paintings of still-life subjects. Analysis based on worksheets and practical exercises in drawing, painting and collage. Set up still life, children make a preliminary drawing. In the second lesson, children elect to do either a painting using the colours they have just been analysing, a line drawing, or a cut-paper collage based on shapes and tones.
Support/extension exercise In sketch books make a drawing of a view from bedroom using either lines, shapes and tones or colour.

....

Lessons 8/9 Analysing the content of an Impressionist painting. Teacher-led discussion of a painting containing figures in a landscape (e.g. Millet's *The gleaners*) examining form, content, process, mood, method. Children analyse a painting of their choice, making written and practical responses through workshop sheet-led activity.
Support/extension exercise Draw a comic strip involving one or more of the characters in the painting.

....

Lessons 8/9 continued Children write and illustrate a short account about the characters in the painting or what might take place in the landscape.

Lesson 10 Gallery visit – children visit gallery for guided tour. Teacher selects and researches one or two paintings prior to the visit. During the visit, teacher conducts form, content, process, mood analysis with children in front of painting. Using worksheet (Teacher activity 6.5), children respond to two paintings of their choice – preferably those also available as postcard reproduction. Back in the classroom the children write about and paint their own version of the painting they analysed – maybe altering the characters, mood, colour scheme, etc.

Lessons 11/12 Teacher-led class discussion analysing the form and content of a painting of a group of people (such as Renoir's 'A dance at the Moulin de la Galette', Plate 1) using work sheet as above. Some children enact a scene from a painting whilst others draw the scene. Repeat twice with different paintings. All children make their own paintings based on their drawings, changing and adapting the context as desired to make a new painting, e.g. the *Moulin de la Galette* becomes a school disco, with blue and red lighting, etc.)

Whole class display Contextual display of the late nineteenth century, providing contextual background for Impressionist-based work and leading to further development in art. Use Parisian photographs, maps of Paris, holiday posters, adverts, nineteenth century costumes and artefacts, photographs of children's ancestors, French song/music/language. Reproductions of Lautrec posters.

Individual summative assessment Each child writes about what they have learned in this scheme based on criteria identified by teacher from lesson objectives.

Figure 6.7 continued

LESSON PLANNING SHEET 1

Aim: To introduce critical studies and to introduce similarities and   **Date** _____   **Class** _____
differences of artefacts broadly classified as art, craft and design.
Learning outcomes: Recognise differences in various types of art, their materials and methods of
making. Begin to talk about art, craft and design. Begin to categorise artefacts.
Whole class . . .   Group . . .   Individuals . . .   Duration 2 hours

Introduction
Teacher Introduce scheme and talk about how we can learn about art from art; introduce term
'critical studies'. Explain that critical means analytical, not adverse comment. Referring to visual
examples, initiate class discussion about the differences between various art, craft and design
objects. Introduce terms, painting, sculpture, photograph, craft objects (print, weaving, pottery,
designed objects), posters/graphics.
Pupil Children respond with questions and discussion, and contribute to blackboard summary.
Resources Pictures, postcards or real objects of a range of different artefacts for discussion.

Development
Teacher Groups of five or six are each given a bundle of about ten postcards, magazine cuttings,
etc. (or some groups use CD-ROM or videodisc), containing a variety of examples of artefacts. Each
group sorts into categories and make short notes to justify their choice.
Pupil Group discussion, classifying and note taking. Mount classified examples and notes on sheet
of A2 sugar paper and display.
Resources Postcards, CD-ROM videodisc player, sugar paper, pencils.

Conclusion
Teacher and pupil Class discussion, spokesperson for each group presents their work to class.
Teacher directs pupils to use appropriate vocabulary in discussing work.
Resources Children's presentation sheets, CD-ROM videodisc, etc.

Formative assessment peer/teacher evaluation as above.
Support/extension exercise Mount in sketch books an example of painting, sculpture, photograph,
craft object and example of designed object.

Figure 6.7 continued

LESSON PLANNING SHEET 2 and 3

Aim: To investigate the similarities and differences between   **Date** _____ **Class** _____
different kinds of painting – still life and landscape.
Learning outcomes: To record what they have experienced through analysing pictures and
drawings, and express ideas confidently; to select primary and secondary sources and experiment
with ideas which are suggested by them; to develop drawing skills and the use of line, tone and
colour. To analyse Impressionist works of art and find connections with their own work.
Whole class . . .   Group . . .   Individuals . . .   Duration 2 + 2 hours

Introduction
Teacher Introduce examples of still-life and landscape painting with reference to Impressionism –
Monet and Cézanne. Discuss reproductions with children, pointing out that not all paintings can be
simply classified as either still life or landscape and that some have elements of each category.
Discuss features of subject, background, composition, etc.
Pupil Respond with questions and discussion, and make drawings in sketch books which
correspond to main features of reproductions being discussed. Class discussion about their work and
the reproductions of artists' work.
Resources Four reproductions of Impressionists' paintings, sketch books, pencils.

Development
Teacher Divide class into six groups, give each group one worksheet identifying the major features
of still life and landscape with questions to respond to by writing and drawing. Give four reproductions
to each group (postcards, posters, books, CD-ROM or videodisc).
Pupil Children write and make pastel drawings based on one landscape and one still life of their
choice.
Resources Reproductions as above, drawing paper, worksheets, pastels, hair spray for fixing
drawings when children have gone. Teacher/pupil discussion of results. Store work safely.

End of first lesson

Lesson 2 and 3 continued

Aim: as before.
Learning outcomes: as before.
Whole class . . .   Group . . .   Individuals . . .   Duration 2 hours

Introduction
Teacher Recap on previous lesson (still life, landscape) and look at work previously completed. Set
up still life similar in style to Cézanne of several boldly shaped objects against a wall. Divide the wall
behind it with drapes and sugar paper; try to achieve a geometric background of harmonious colour
and shape. Clear a space in front of a window so that children can draw the view beyond. Discuss
with children the composition of the still life and also the major shapes and features seen both within
the still life and in the landscape seen from the window.

Figure 6.7 continued

Development
Teacher and pupil Divide children into two groups, 'still life artists', and 'landscape artists'. Children make large pastel drawings from observation concentrating on bold shapes and colours. Teacher helps children by identifying in their work main compositional features – shapes of objects, geometric background divisions, shapes of buildings, windows, chimneys, landscape, sky. Remind them that, as in the artist's work they have analysed, the background is as important as the foreground.
Resources Objects for still life, cloth, drapes, drawing boards and clips if possible, A2 sugar paper, pastels, chalks, hair spray, aprons.

....

Conclusion
Teacher Help children to display work.
Pupil Children display own work and reproductions on wall, together with their writing and analytical drawings of artists' work on still life and landscape. If possible, use still life objects as part of the display and mount landscape drawings adjacent to windows.
Resources Paper for mounting drawings, drapes, objects, etc.

....

Formative assessment/support/extension exercise Children make written evaluations of their own work using criteria identified by the teacher from lesson objectives.

classroom before the visit, and indicate follow-up work after the visit to incorporate what has been experienced into the child's future practical work.

SUMMARY

This Unit has linked theory to practice by revisiting the important values and issues discussed within the book, and suggested ways in which they can be incorporated in practical classroom activities. The central features of visual literacy and critical studies have been discussed with reference to theoretical structures, research findings and the work of children and a practising artist. Importantly, for classroom teaching the relationship between visual literacy and critical studies has been made explicit in both schemes and lessons.

The philosophy, theory, models and methods of evaluation and assessment of children's art work have been outlined. To support the relationship between formative assessment and the process of the children's art making, sample teacher questions have been devised to frame conversation with the child. Classroom display has been incorporated within assessment as a suitable vehicle for formative evaluation and summative celebration of children's work. Suggestions for differentiated work have been given in support and extension exercises.

The sample schemes and lessons have been offered not just for their content but as models for systematic planning. This planning is further supported by material in the resource section.

The final Unit gives teachers the opportunity to reflect on their development in relation to the theory and practices of art education.

Unit 7

On reflection

In this Unit, an audit of what has been proposed and some suggestions for further professional development in primary art teaching are made in order to re-emphasise the need for reflective practice in art education.

THE RELATIONSHIP BETWEEN ART, THE INDIVIDUAL AND SOCIETY

In contemplating the relationship between art and society, the involvement of the individual person must be central. It is from this central position that issues concerned with teaching must emanate, because although teaching is a social activity, children learn individually. This also applies to teachers, and professional development must ultimately depend on an individual's reflection on their own practice.

To envisage a society without art is as meaningless as to envisage art devoid of its social context. In his book *The Story of Art*, Gombrich says:

 We do not know how art began anymore than we know how language started. If we take art to mean such activities as building temples and houses, making pictures and sculptures, or weaving patterns there is no people in all the world without art.

(Gombrich 1972: 19)

This book has stressed the importance of learning about art from art. We have recommended looking in depth at paintings, sculpture and artefacts, but teachers can also learn about art from listening to children, as we have listened to Joseph, Susan and Tom. Further, teachers can learn from listening to artists, as we have through extracts from Millet, Victor Passmore, Roger Fry and Alan Richards. Here, Alan talks about his relationship to art, and the way that ideas come to him from experience and are developed in his paintings:

There used to be a man in Cornwall who sat upon the cliffs and when he saw the shoals of pilchards he would shout, 'Heava, heava!' and then the boats would go out to that particular point. Now I imagined that I wanted to do a painting of a cliff, this place near Perranporth which is kind of dramatic, and I thought, what would it be like to be that man, how would he see the world? And I imagined him looking up at the sky and day dreaming, and he would see a mackerel sky, so I painted mackerel in the sky. And sometimes when there are shoals of fish you can smell the fish can't you, so I imagined the waves turning into fish. So that's what is behind the picture, its not just a landscape, it has all that in it.

As a teacher you will readily recognise the ease of imagination shown by Alan. Many children share this ability to look at an ordinary experience and invest it with elaborated detail drawn from their imagination. It is the mark of an artist that he or she can keep this active imagination alive. As a teacher you are used to devising activities for children that are designed to foster and develop the imagination, for example leaving a story unfinished and asking the children to suggest an ending, or giving them a magazine cutting of an event and asking them to write about what might be happening. We suggest that there are many opportunities for developing children's imagination in relation to art, through affording them the chance to listen to artists.

Artists often are very articulate about their art making and reading their notebooks, journals, letters and articles as well as watching videos, can inform and enlighten as well as inspire. We can gain a sense of the relationship between the artist and their art, of how they draw their inspiration from their experience, and how they use media to reveal their intention.

ART AND ART TEACHING

Although this book has been largely concerned with practical issues related to art education and to teaching and learning, the thread running through these topics has been the necessity to understand the nature of the subject and to demystify its more esoteric characteristics.

It is not necessary for teachers to become artists in order to teach art, but it is necessary for them to develop insights into how artists think, and if possible develop similar ways of thinking. It could be that this is eventually of more use in the classroom than acquiring technical skills in a particular medium, although, of course, this is also of immense benefit.

In our experience, the way most primary teachers think and feel demonstrates reassuring similarities between them and artists. Both are aware that invention and creativity can only be developed and brought to a successful conclusion through clear strategies, logical developments and manageable procedures. Artists and teachers are also well aware that effort and tenacity are both necessary for successful work, whether it is achieving a teaching or learning objective or bringing a painting or sculpture to fruition.

All successful activities demand a high level of engagement. This is so in making art and teaching it. A difficulty that most people have in making a drawing is to put the first marks down on the huge, white sheet of paper. Similarly, in teaching, the first few moments of letting children loose with paint, glue and scissors can be an anxious moment. However, once the initial moves have been made then developing the drawing or the lesson becomes

Figure 7.1 Painting takes time, care and commitment

more straightforward as the individual becomes engaged in the activity. Sometimes, in the middle period of a lesson or a drawing, confidence is required to develop exciting and original work. It could be argued that this confidence is as important as possessing the necessary craft skills and knowledge.

Teaching is an art not just a technical procedure, although of course it has technical procedures within it. Teaching is interactive, involving professional judgements, and in our experience, despite some current orthodoxy, learning is not 'delivered' like bottles of milk, nor is learning acquired by simply receiving it. The development of ideas and techniques is a reciprocal process. This is true of teaching and art making. Creative intervention and management of the process is needed, both by the teacher and the artist, if there is to be a successful outcome.

The relationship between engagement and confidence is a matter of knowledge and understanding as well as experience. They grow together. We hope that the teacher activities, suggestions for schemes and lessons, and the perspective on art history and criticism, will increase teachers' confidence. We have employed the strategies of reflective practice and group discussion in the belief that these techniques will promote engagement with the issues, as well as initiate practical programmes of teaching and learning.

Conversations about art and art education are recommended, because developing a language for art is both a means to increase insight and understanding about the subject and a tool for talking to children about their work (including formative and summative assessment). Language should always be used to enlighten, not to impress or mystify.

THE TEACHER AS PRACTITIONER

In reading and taking part in the activities in this book you will already have carried out some practical activities. Whereas we have asserted that enthusiasm, engagement and an openness to the experience are more important than highly developed technical skills, we also understand that a lack of confidence in techniques and handling of materials can prevent a teacher introducing such skills to children.

In Unit 5 we suggested some strategies that schools might employ in planning for staff development in art teaching. In our experience there is always somebody in a primary school who is interested in art and who will be willing to take on the role of art co-ordinator. Part of this role will be a willingness to learn more about the practical skills of art making and, given the possible breadth of an art curriculum, this is no mean task. Such skills might include:

- drawing
- painting
- printmaking
- collage
- three-dimensional work in clay, box-work, wire and plaster sculpture
- textiles – surface embroidery, weaving, appliqué, batik, soft sculpture
- design-related activities linked with technology
- computer aided drawing
- photography
- handwriting
- critical studies

A school might select from this list the core activities of drawing and painting and some three-dimensional work (preferably clay), and then plan a programme supported by critical studies that will develop these core activities over the years. They can then select from the remaining list activities that can be focused on and developed throughout the primary years, to enrich and support learning in the core activities.

An art co-ordinator should ideally have a developed understanding of the techniques and processes needed in the use of a range of media and be in a position to guide other teachers in the handling of these materials. It takes time to build this knowledge and understanding, and part of the school's planning for staff development should acknowledge the need to build in a programme of staff training, led by the co-ordinator, art advisory teacher or County Advisor. Once this programme is in place, the staff can gradually build their confidence alongside their practical skills. Should this not be immediately possible, we recommend a do-it-yourself strategy outlined in the following teacher activity.

The strategy depends on the notion already outlined in this book, that a teacher can learn a great deal about materials, equipment and media by working alongside the children in their classes. This needs a positive attitude on the part of the teacher and a willingness to acknowledge that they do not always need to know everything about a subject in order to be a good teacher.

Children welcome an opportunity to learn alongside a teacher and share what they discover in an equal way, and this joint learning offers an authentic and professionally credible way of teaching and learning. In Plate 16 the children have explored a new way of mask making with their teacher.

The activity below is intended to offer a model for building confidence in handling and teaching any medium.

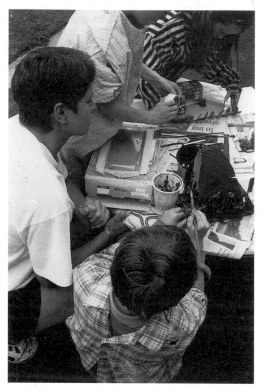

Figure 7.2 Teachers can learn alongside children

 TEACHER ACTIVITY 7.1

Plan to work alongside one or two colleagues in this activity, which is designed to build your confidence in using a new medium and technique. With your colleague choose one art activity that you would like to teach children but of which you have little or no experience yourself. Follow the 'action steps' listed below using a notepad to log your actions, thoughts and feelings.

Tick the factors that make you nervous about teaching the children how to use this medium:

(a) Never used it myself.
(b) Used it once and had a disaster.
(c) Don't know what it is like, how it behaves, how to control it.
(d) Don't know how to develop this media through a process.
(e) Don't know what to use it for.
(f) Don't know how to ascertain what children can learn by using it.
(g) Don't know how to organise teaching it.

(h) Not sure of what vocabulary or terminology to use in relation to it.

(i) Not sure how to link the practical work with the work of artists, crafts persons or designers.

Talk and make notes about any of these factors influencing you and then select from the following self-help strategies to find a way forward.

Research

Borrow adults' or children's books from the library that describe the use of the medium. Make notes that will be of future use to other colleagues and the children. Also research artists, crafts persons or designers who may have used this medium in their work. Collect visual material and make notes to form a resource for the school. Include in these notes a glossary of terms that apply to the medium or the processes that develop the medium. (A short glossary is included in this book, page 137.)

Learning through experiments with the medium

Arrange a time after school when you and your colleagues can experiment with the medium in order to find out some answers to factors (c), (d) and (e) above. Allow yourself at least three-quarters of an hour to handle the medium and make notes about its nature, what it can do and how it behaves. As you experiment, ideas will occur to you about how to use this medium to make something and how you might develop this through a process. This will give you some ideas about factors (d) and (e).

Learning about the formal elements of art

Refer to the National Curriculum attainment targets in Unit 2 (Figures 2.4 (page 31) and 2.5 (page 32)). What can you say about the medium in relation to the formal elements of colour, line, pattern, texture, tone, shape, and form? Will it be appropriate to develop the children's understanding of all these elements through the use of this medium or will the medium lend itself to particular elements rather than others? Answers to these questions will also inform you about the potential of children's ability to learn about the formal elements.

Planning some lessons

Refer to the lesson planning suggestions in Unit 6 and plan at least four lessons that would develop the use of this medium and would allow children both to experiment, and to apply their understanding of the medium to an idea which would lead to an end product.

Children's learning

Re-read Barnes' guidelines in Unit 6 (page 90) and apply each of the categories to your lesson plans. Carefully identify how you would evaluate and assess the children's work based on this criteria.

After the lessons have been taught, meet with your colleagues again, look at the children's work and discuss the children's learning. Re-read your initial notes. In particular, refer back to your initial feelings of confidence in teaching the medium and your knowledge and understanding of it, and compare them to your current views. Discuss with your colleagues how to disseminate your increased knowledge and understanding to other members of staff and plan accordingly.

REAFFIRMING THE NOTION OF REFLECTIVE PRACTICE IN ART

The last teacher activity will have directly involved you and your colleagues in reflecting on your practice. In the introduction we suggested that the idea of using this book was to:

Read about it – a topic, an issue, an idea.
Do it – a practical activity or discussion.
Talk about it – review and analyse what has been carried out and discussed.
Plan – develop strategies for future action.
Do some more!

Embodied in this is the notion of active learning – not a series of prescriptive recipes for teaching art to primary children. Furthermore, this approach places the teacher's professional judgement at the centre of the learning process.

In writing this book we have frequently used the metaphor of the journey to describe various processes. Terms such as routes, maps, looking backward and looking forward have consistently featured. We have also referred to touchstones as a way of connecting art with the exterior world and the landscape of our feeling and imagination. There are many ways of traversing the territory of primary art education, consequently we do not suggest one perfect map but instead ways in which teachers, in agreement with their colleagues, might find their own sure-footed route, appropriate to their needs.

The National Curriculum gives all children an entitlement to art education but the quality of what is taught and learned will depend on the teacher. We agree wholeheartedly with David Best, who states, 'The most important areas of education require sensitive, informed judgment, and thus there can never be a substitute for high quality teachers' (Best 1992: 34).

Sensitive, informed judgement is developed through reflective practice. In this book we have adopted a structure of reflection on practice as a basis for professional learning and development. It is our hope that the good practice we have observed in primary schools will be developed further by teachers committed to affirming the qualities embodied in art – inventive, imaginative and unique ways of making sense of the world.

Resources section

GALLERY VISIT WORKSHEET

1   Name of painting ....

2   Name of artist   3   Date of work ....

4   Medium/media   5   Landscape ☐   Still life ☐   Portrait ☐

6   Description of the picture ....

....

....

7   Sketch the picture in this box.   8   List the main colours in this box.

9   Describe the light and shade – which direction does the light seem to come from? ....

....

....

10   Describe the mood created in the painting. ....

....

11   What else can you find out about the artist/painting? ....

....

....

....

GALLERY VISIT WORKSHEET

1   Choose a painting you like and look at it carefully. Look at the colours and the shapes. Look at the marks and the texture. Look at the details.

2   Draw the picture in this box.

3   Are there any people in the picture? What are they doing? ....

....

4   What is the most important thing in this painting? What has the artist done to make it seem important? ....

....

5   When you look at the painting, how do your eyes travel round the work? List the journey your eyes make. ....

6   List the colours the artist has used. ....

What is the *main* colour in the picture? ....

7   How has the painter shown the effect of light in this picture? From which direction is the light coming? ....

8   Put a circle round the number that best describes the picture (e.g. very warm would be 1, very cold would be 5).

WARM	1	2	3	4	5	COLD
CALM	1	2	3	4	5	BUSY
DULL	1	2	3	4	5	BRIGHT
ROUGH	1	2	3	4	5	SMOOTH
GENTLE	1	2	3	4	5	ANGRY

9   Follow-up activities:
(a) Back at school create your own picture of the same subject. Try to use some of the ideas that the artist used, such as the same colours, mood, brush marks.
(b) Write a story or a poem about the picture based on your memory of the details. Use your sketch to refresh your memory.
(c) Script a play for you and your friends based on the picture. You can use the picture as a starting point for the play and use your imagination to work out what will happen next.
(d) Visit the library to find out more about the artist. Make notes about the artist's paintings, their life and times.

RESOURCES FOR ART TEACHING

Reproduction of paintings

Catalogues can be obtained from:

The Shorewood Collection
Mainstone Publications
Sparham
Norwich
NR9 5AQ

Folens Publishers
Albert House
Apex Business Centre
Boscombe Road
Dunstable
LU5 4RL

Slides, slide sets and films

Visual Publications
The Green
Northleach
Cheltenham
GL54 3EX

Budek
Pelham Street
Newport
Rhode Island
02840 USA

CD-ROM

Marshall Cavendish
PO Box 1
Hastings
TN35 4TJ

Schools Direct
The Green
Ravensthorpe
Northampton
NN6 8EP

Video tape

The Shell Education Service (free loan
service/thematic content for schools)
Shell UK Ltd
Shell-Mex House
Strand
London WC2

TVS Education (Art of the Western World
Art and design education resource pack to
improve teachers' subject knowledge)
Television Centre
Southampton
SO9 5HZ

Video and Film Production (British art in
the twentieth century – teachers' subject
knowledge and notes for lessons)
Corporate Communications Services
The British Petroleum Company PLC
Britannic House
1 Finsbury Circus
London
EC2M 7BA

Roland Collection (Films and videos on art
and artists – teacher subject knowledge
and visual material for children)
Peasmarsh
East Sussex
TN31 6XJ

Galleries and museums

Obtainable from the education
departments at major galleries: books,
slide packs, resource materials for visits,
thematic materials, postcards, posters.

National Gallery
Trafalgar Square
London
WC2N 5DN

Hatching This is a form of shading made by drawing parallel lines. *Cross-hatching* is made by one layer of parallel lines crossing another layer at right angles.

Icon An object or image in which special meaning has been invested by the viewer or society (e.g. religious symbols, coca-cola bottles).

Line The basic element of drawing, with many different qualities and characteristics – straight, curved, heavy, broken, etc. Line can indicate structure and form as well as simple outline of shape.

Medium, media The materials used by an artist – for painters, paint is their medium; for ceramicists, clay. A *mixed-media* piece is made up of two or more media.

Narrative Paintings that in their subject matter tell a story or part of a story can be described as narrative. Similarly, this term can also be used to describe certain pottery, sculpture, textiles or prints that have a narrative theme.

Negative space The spaces in between major objects or people in a picture. Sometimes referred to as 'ground' as in 'figure and ground relationship'.

Pattern The arrangement of repeated shapes or marks in a regular (e.g. a brick wall) or irregular manner (e.g. pebbles on a beach).

Perspective A convention that describes three-dimensional space on a two-dimensional surface. Invented in fifteenth century Europe, it uses a system in which parallel lines lead the eye toward a point on the horizon known as the 'vanishing point'. Many artists in the twentieth century, including abstract artists, have become disinterested in perspective as a convention and create a feeling or illusion of space in a different way. Primary children become interested in perspective in the upper junior years after exploring a range of intelligent approaches to portraying space through base lines/sky lines, X-ray drawings, plan and elevation, overlapping, etc. They will need introducing to perspective by their teacher. *Aerial perspective* is concerned with portraying distance by using colours and tones. Objects in the foreground appear near (by using 'hot' colours such as reds and oranges, or maximum tonal contrast), objects in the middle distance appear to be further off (mid-tones), and objects in the distance appear far away (by using 'cool' colours such as pale blues or a range of pale greys, or very pale tones).

Scale Scale describes the relative size of an object in comparison to another object. Young children pay little attention to actual scale in their art work, drawing what is most important to them largest. As children mature, they come to appreciate how to represent scale in their work and also how to portray this using comparative size (e.g. Michael's drawing of the sunflower, page 47). They also begin to draw things that they 'know' are large objects smaller in relation to other objects, 'because they are far away'.

Shape Something flat and two-dimensional.

Style Represents the main characteristics of a given group of artists as well as that of an individual artist. Identifying a particular style allows us to make profitable analysis of an individual's work as well as talk in broad terms about work produced by a country or period.

Texture The quality of surfaces, that can be both seen and felt. Representations of textured surfaces can be made in drawing, painting, collage, etc.

Tone The degree of lightness or darkness. The concept of tone in relation to black and white is easier for children to understand. The tonal value of colour is more difficult, but can be explained through work on tonal contrasts; for example, yellow looks lighter in tone than blue; red looks darker in tone than orange. Black and white photocopying of colour work can identify the tonal differences of colour very well.

Visual elements of art Line, shape, texture, tone, pattern, colour and form.

References

Abbs, P. (1989) *A is for Aesthetic: Essays on creative and aesthetic education*, New York: Falmer Press.

Arnheim, R. (1954) *Art and Visual Perception*, London: University of California Press.

Barnes, R. (1987) *Teaching Art to Young Children*, London: Allen and Unwin.

Bennett, N. and Carré, C. (1989) 'Primary teachers and the National Curriculum', in *Research Papers in Education* 14, 3: 17–46.

Bennett, N. and Carré, C. (1993) *Learning to Teach*, London: Routledge.

Best, D. (1992) *The Rationality of Feeling*, London: Falmer Press.

Best, D. (1995) *Feeling and Reason in the Arts*, London: Allen and Unwin.

Booth, D. (1977) 'Pattern painting by the young child', in J. Goodnow *Children's Drawing*, London: Fontana.

Britton, J. (1980) *Language and Learning*, Harmondsworth: Penguin Books.

Champkin, J. (1992) 'Naming a well-known artist' in the *Daily Mail*: London.

Clement, R. (1986) *The Art Teacher's Handbook*, London: Hutchinson.

D.E.S. (1991) *National Curriculum Art Working Group: Interim Report*, London: D.E.S.

D.F.E. (1995) *Art in the National Curriculum*, D.F.E.: London.

Eisner, E. (1972) 'Educating artistic vision', in R. Barnes *Teaching Art to Young Children*, London: Allen and Unwin.

Fairbairn, A. (1987) *Design and Primary Education*, London: The Design Council.

Goldwater, R. and Treves, M. (eds) *Artists on Art*, London: John Murray.

Gombrich, E. (1972) *The Story of Art*, London: Phaidon Press.

Goodnow, J. (1977) *Children's Drawing*, London: Fontana.

Hogben, C. (1978) *The Art of Bernard Leach*, London: Faber and Faber.

Hughes, R. (1991) *The Shock of the New*, London: BBC Publications.

Jacobus, J. (1963) *World Architecture: Illustrated History*, London: Paul Hamlyn.

Keith-Lucas (1980) 'Design education at secondary level', in Fairbairn, *Design and Primary Education*, London: Design Council.

Kellog, R. (1969) *Analysing Children's Art*, Palo Alto, California: National Press.

Kemmis, S. (1982) *The Action Research Planner*, Victoria: Geelong Deakin University Press.

Lambirth, A. (1993) 'Taking stock', in *Royal Academy Magazine*, 41: Winter.

Lowenfeld, V. and Brittain, W.L. (1987 edition) *Creative and Mental Growth*, New York: Macmillan.

Matthews, J. (1987) 'The young child's early representation and drawing', in M. Geva and A. Kelly *Early Childhood Education*, London: Paul Chapman.

OFSTED (1993) *Curriculum Organisation and Classroom Practice in Primary Schools: A follow-up report*, London: OFSTED.

Parsons, M. (1987) *How We Understand Art*, Cambridge: Cambridge University Press.

Pollard, A. and Tann, S. (1987) *Reflective Teaching in the Primary School*, London: Cassell.

Reid, L. (1973) 'Aesthetics and aesthetic education', in D. Field and J. Newick (eds) *The Study of Education and Art*, London: Routledge and Kegan Paul.

Ruskin, J. (1857) 'Elements of drawing', in H. Read *Education through Art* (1958), London: Faber and Faber.

Taylor, R. (1986) *Educating for Art*, Essex: Longman.

Taylor, R. and Andrews, G. (1993) *The Arts in the Primary School*, London: Falmer Press.

Treacher, V. (ed.) *Assessment and Evaluation in the Arts*, Reading: Berkshire Education Authority.

Walter, J. (1995) 'Ioanna Constantinidis', in *Ceramic Review* 152: April.

Willig, C. (1990) *Children's Concepts and the Primary Curriculum*, London: Paul Chapman.

Index